D0779259

Academic Dishonesty
An Educator's Guide

♦ ♦ ♦

Academic Dishonesty
An Educator's Guide

♦ ♦ ♦

Bernard E. Whitley, Jr.
Patricia Keith-Spiegel
Ball State University

LAWRENCE ERLBAUM ASSOCIATES, PUBLISHERS
2002   Mahwah, NJ   London

Copyright © 2002 by Lawrence Erlbaum Associates, Inc.
All rights reserved. No part of this book may be reproduced in any form, by photostat, microform, retrieval system, or any other means, without prior written permission of the publisher.

Lawrence Erlbaum Associates, Inc., Publishers
10 Industrial Avenue
Mahwah, NJ 07430

Cover design by Patricia Keith-Spiegel

Library of Congress Cataloging-in-Publication Data

Whitley, Bernard E.
Academic dishonesty : an educator's guide / Bernard E. Whitley, Jr., and Patricia Keith-Spiegel.
    p. cm.
Includes bibliographical references and index.
ISBN 0-8058-4019-2 (cloth : alk. paper)
ISBN 0-8058-4020-6 (pbk. : alk. paper)
1. Cheating (Education) 2. College students—Conduct of life.
   3. College discipline. I. Keith-Spiegel, Patricia. II. Title.
LB3609 .W45 2001
378.1'958—dc21   2001023819
                                              CIP

Books published by Lawrence Erlbaum Associates are printed on acid-free paper, and their bindings are chosen for strength and durability.

Printed in the United States of America
10 9 8 7 6 5 4 3 2 1

Contents

◆ ◆ ◆

III   Academic Integrity as an Institutional Issue

Preface

◆ ◆ ◆

- Why do students cheat?
- What can be done to prevent it?
- What are the consequences of ignoring academic dishonesty?
- How should suspected students be confronted?
- What sanctions are appropriate for students who violate the academic honesty policy?
- What can the institution do to encourage a campus ethos of integrity?

Our goal is to provide readers with a concise handbook covering the full spectrum of issues related to academic dishonesty. To do so, we present research and theory on academic dishonesty and strategies for preventing, confronting, and managing the problem.

The book is divided into three parts. The first part reviews the existing published literature about academic dishonesty among college and university students and how faculty members respond to the problem. Chapter 1 addresses the issues of why academic dishonesty is an important problem in academia, the prevalence of the problem, the rationalizations some instructors use to minimize its importance or deny its existence, and some of the real difficulties involved in confronting the problem. In chapter 2, we focus on definitions of academic dishonesty and how student and faculty differ in their perceptions of what behaviors constitute academic dishonesty. This chapter also describes the reasons and justifications students give for their dishonest acts, some of the institutional and student characteristics associated with academic dishonesty, and a theoretical model that helps explain the conditions under which cheating is most likely to occur.

The second part of the book presents practical advice designed to help college and university instructors and administrators deal proactively and effectively with academic dishonesty. Chapter 3 offers techniques for fostering academic integrity in the classroom. Chapter 4 presents techniques that are helpful in preventing academic dishonesty from occurring. Chapter 5 presents methods of detecting academic dishonesty, and also discusses the difficult problem of confronting and dealing with students suspected of cheating. The last part, chapter 6, considers the broader question of academic integrity as a system-wide issue within institutions of higher education.

Because our topic is academic dishonesty, we may appear to be taking on an adversarial "us against them" attitude toward students. That is definitely not our perspective. We know that a great many students value their educations and work diligently to learn. These are the students who make our jobs joyful. Indeed, part of our own interests in the nature, prevention, detection, and remediation of academic dishonesty stems from our commitment to the welfare of honest students. Cheaters *do* hurt themselves, but they do not *only* hurt themselves: They also degrade the education of and affront the integrity of their honest peers. We believe that the best way to pay our respects to honest students is to be actively involved in maintaining a climate of integrity in the classroom and throughout the entire campus. We have written this book to help others serve their students, their colleges and universities, and the academic community in that way.

As we were completing this book, we found an article describing the problem of academic dishonesty in high schools (Bushweller, 1999) and were struck by the similarities of the problem in the high school and college/university contexts. Although we are college instructors and wrote this book with the college/university context in mind, we believe that the principles we describe are also applicable to the high school environment. We are aware that implementing our suggestions in the high school environment raises issues, such as the fact that almost all high school students are minors, which college and university faculty and administrators do not face. Nonetheless, as Bushweller has shown, appropriate academic integrity policies can be developed and implemented in high schools with positive educational effects. We hope that our book can provide some ideas that high school faculty and administrators find useful.

ACKNOWLEDGMENTS

We extend our deep appreciation to our reviewers for their many suggestions and comments: Stephen F. Davis, Emporia State University; Marci Gaither, Ball State University; Terry Greene, Franklin and Marshall

College; Lisa Gray-Shellberg, California State University, Dominguez Hills; Joe Kerkvliet, Oregon State University; Donald McCabe, Rutgers, The State University of New Jersey–Newark; and Gary Pavela, University of Maryland at College Park. In addition, we thank Jennifer Padgett and Benjamin Vold for providing a student's perspective of the book.

—*Bernard E. Whitley*
—*Patricia Keith-Spiegel*

I

Definitions, Incidence, Research, and Theory

1

Academic Dishonesty:
The Enemy Within Our Gates

◆ ◆ ◆

The university at the undergraduate level sounds like a place where cheating comes almost as naturally as breathing, where it's an academic skill almost as important as reading, writing and math. —*Moffatt (1990, p. 2)*

Moffatt's view may strike many readers as overly cynical, but there is a growing recognition that academic dishonesty is a major problem on college campuses (e.g., Maramark & Maline, 1993) and increasing numbers of students are engaging in it (e.g., Collison, 1990; Peyser, 1992). These concerns have been reinforced by the publication of how-to books on cheating, such as Corbett's (1999) *The Cheater's Handbook* and the establishment of what might be called *cheaters' sites* on the World Wide Web (WWW). Collectively, these sites provide thousands of term papers and examinations (e.g., Hickman, 1998; McCollum, 1996).

Although Fass (1990) attributed high levels of contemporary academic dishonesty among college students to their having been "raised in an era of decline in public morality" (p. 171), cheating and other forms of academic dishonesty are not new problems. These behaviors have existed as long as there have been tests and will probably continue as long as students are evaluated. Brickman (1961) noted that attempts at cheating were so common during the ancient Chinese civil service examinations that candidates were searched for crib notes and confined to individual examination rooms for the duration of the examination (usually 3 days) to prevent collaboration. The government further attempted to discourage cheating by imposing the death penalty on cheaters. Despite these precautions, examination candidates still tried to cheat, such as by having concealed pockets sewn into their clothing in which crib notes could be hidden.

EIGHT REASONS THAT EDUCATORS SHOULD BE
CONCERNED ABOUT ACADEMIC INTEGRITY

Why should we, as faculty members and administrators, be concerned about cheating and other forms of academic dishonesty? There are eight reasons.

   1. Equity. Students who cheat may be getting higher grades than they deserve. For example, a survey of high school teachers found that 58% believed that cheating is partly responsible for grade inflation (Bushweller, 1999). In addition, when student grades are assigned on the basis of the average score in the class or other norm-referenced means, students who do not cheat may get lower grades than they deserve whenever cheaters raise the class average. Teachers have an essential ethical responsibility to treat their students fairly (Keith-Spiegel, Wittig, Perkins, Balogh, & Whitley, 1993); failure to deal with academic dishonesty is a violation of this ethical obligation. Both instructors and students view a college teacher's ignoring evidence of academic dishonesty as a severe ethical violation (Morgan, Korschgen, & Gardner, 1996; Tabachnick, Keith-Spiegel, & Pope, 1991).

   2. Character development. Moral and ethical development of students is an important mission of higher education (e.g., Dalton, 1985; Kibler, 1993a; Kibler, Nuss, Paterson, & Pavela, 1988)—one that has been endorsed by the U. S. legal system in its decisions on legal challenges to institutional disciplinary actions in cases of academic dishonesty (Kibler et al., 1988). Although many faculty members, especially those at research-oriented universities, no longer see student character or moral development as part of their calling (e.g., Sandeen, 1985), faculty responses to academic dishonesty can strongly influence students' personal development. When students see other students cheating and do not see faculty members and administrators addressing such behavior, they may decide that academic dishonesty is acceptable or at least permissible. Because norms supportive of academic dishonesty tend to encourage such behavior (Whitley, 1998), faculty and administration that appear unconcerned about it may reinforce any such norms that already exist (Gehring & Pavela, 1994). Conversely, a normative context that eschews academic dishonesty, such as the existence of an honor system, tends to discourage the behavior (McCabe & Trevino, 1993; McCabe, Trevino, & Butterfield, 1999).

3. *The mission to transfer knowledge.* Central missions of every institution of higher education are preservation and search for knowledge, transmission of that knowledge to a new generation of citizens and scholars, and personal, social, cultural, and intellectual development of the members of the college or university community. Students who cheat their way through the higher education system do not acquire the knowledge to which their degrees are supposed to attest nor do they engage in the intellectual and moral struggles that foster personal development (Gehring & Pavela, 1994). Toleration of academic dishonesty, therefore, diminishes the intellectual and moral capital required by society for its common development and progress.

4. *Student morale.* When honest students see some of their peers cheat and get away with it, especially if it appears that instructors do not seem to care, they become frustrated and angry (e.g, Jendrek, 1992). Seeing other students gain the same rewards for cheating as they do for effort may lead them to become disenchanted with and cynical about higher education. These negative emotions may, in turn, lower honest students' motivation to learn. Some students may abandon effort as a success strategy and come to view cheating as the only way to keep up with everyone else.

5. *Faculty morale.* Faculty members who learn that students have cheated in their classes often feel personally violated and mistreated by their students, reacting with feelings of anger and disgust (e.g., Jendrek, 1989; Johnston, 1996). Instructors also describe dealing with cheating as one of the most stressful aspects of their jobs (Keith-Spiegel, Tabachnick, Whitley, & Washburn, 1998). These negative emotions can be compounded by perceptions that administrators do not support their efforts to control academic dishonesty and punish cheaters (e.g., Schneider, 1999; Wilson, 1998). Over time, these emotions can result in cynical attitudes toward students, administrators, and the educational process (e.g., Schneider, 1999).

6. *Students' future behavior.* Students who cheat in college frequently go on to cheat in graduate and professional school and to engage in unethical business practices (e.g., Baldwin, Daugherty, Rowley, & Schwarz, 1996; Sims, 1993). Because having successfully cheated at the undergraduate and graduate levels can make it easier to cheat in one's professional career, failure to deal adequately with academic dishonesty and educate students about the consequences of their behavior constitutes a disservice not only to the academic community but to society in general. In contrast, students who have been held to high academic ethics standards as undergraduates

are less likely to commit ethical violations in the workplace (McCabe, Trevino, & Butterfield, 1996).

7. *Reputation of the institution.* Incidents of academic dishonesty, especially when they involve the collaboration of many students (e.g, a "cheating ring") or an odd feature (e.g., a student's attempt to blackmail an instructor unless copies of upcoming examinations were supplied), are of interest to the media. The name of the institution is prominently linked with the dishonest activity, and such associations can sully, at least temporarily, its reputation. Should an institution experience frequent, publicized incidents of academic dishonesty, its reputation may be more permanently tarnished. *The Chronicle of Higher Education,* widely read in academic circles, regularly reports unusual incidents of academic dishonesty among students and faculty, such as the case at the University of Minnesota in which a staff member in the athletics department routinely wrote papers for varsity athletes (Lords, 2000). Occasionally, the publicity reaches the popular press. One example was the 1993 incident at the U.S. Naval Academy in which an estimated 160 midshipmen were believed to have received advanced copies of a final examination. A *Newsweek* headline read, "A growing cheating scandal raises new questions about how the military trains its officer" (Glick & Turque, 1993).

8. *Public confidence in higher education.* The effects of failing to address academic dishonesty contribute to a broader problem: the public's growing lack of confidence in the academy as illustrated by such professor-bashing books as Anderson's (1992) *Impostors in the Temple,* Cahn's (1994) *Saints and Scamps: Ethics in Academia,* and Sykes' (1988) *ProfScam: Professors and the Demise of Higher Education.* Students who cheat, those who see others successfully cheat, those who hear others brag about how they cheated their way through college, and employers who find themselves with incompetent and dishonest employees cannot help but lose faith in academia. Such loss of faith can easily lead to loss of support for higher education.

ACADEMIC DISHONESTY TODAY

The best data on the prevalence of academic dishonesty come from a survey conducted by McCabe and Trevino (1993) of 6,096 undergraduate students at 31 institutions of higher education in the United States. The survey included both institutions with honor codes and those without. The two types of schools were matched on enrollment and academic selectivity as indicated by students' mean SAT scores. To be classified as an honor code institution, a school had to meet at least two of the following criteria: unproctored examinations, an honor pledge, a requirement for student reporting of honor code violations, and the existence of a student court or peer judiciary board that ruled on alleged honor code violations. Most of the honor code institutions surveyed met at least three of these criteria.

McCabe and Trevino (1993) asked their respondents to indicate how frequently they had engaged in each of the 12 behaviors listed in Table 1.1 during their college careers. Table 1.2 shows the percentage of students who reported engaging in at least 1 of the 12 behaviors at least once. Table 1.2 also shows the percentages of students who reported engaging in each of three categories of behavior at least once: cheating on examinations, cheating on homework assignments, and plagiarism. Overall, almost three quarters of the students reported engaging in some form of academic dishonesty during their college careers, about half reported having cheated on examinations or having plagiarized, and slightly less than half reported having cheated on homework assignments. Cheating rates at institutions with honor codes were almost half those at other institutions. Nonetheless, more than half the students at honor code schools reported having engaged in some form of academic dishonesty, and one quarter to almost one third reported having engaged in each of the specific forms of dishonesty.

Disturbingly, a substantial number of students are repeat cheaters. Hollinger and Lanza-Kaduce (1996) found that 21% of the students in their sample admitted to at least three incidents of cheating while in college, with 9% admitting to six or more incidents. McCabe and Trevino (1995) found that 38% of their respondents admitted to three or more cheating incidents. Defining repeat cheating in a slightly different way, Moffatt (1990) found that 33% of the students in his sample admitted to having cheated in eight or more courses in college. If one assumes that a typical student takes about 40 courses in college (5 per semester), Moffatt's data mean that one student in three cheats in at least 8 of those courses during a college career.

THE COLLEGE INSTRUCTOR AND
ACADEMIC DISHONESTY

Between 60% and 80% of faculty members report having been faced with instances of academic dishonesty (Graham, Monday, O'Brien, & Steffen, 1994; Jendrek, 1989; McCabe & Trevino, 1995; Singhal, 1982). However,

TABLE 1.1
Forms of Academic Dishonesty Assessed in McCabe and Trevino's (1993) Survey

Using crib notes on a test

Copying from another student during a test

Using unfair methods to learn what was on a test before it was given

Copying from another student during a test without his or her knowledge

Helping someone else cheat on a test

Cheating on a test in any other way

Copying material and turning it in as your own work

Fabricating or falsifying a bibliography

Turning in work done by someone else

Receiving substantial, unpermitted help on an assignment

Collaborating on an assignment when the instructor asked for individual work

Copying a few sentences of material from a published source without footnoting it

---

a substantial minority of instructors appear to be reluctant to do anything about it (Schneider, 1999): Between 3% and 21% of faculty members report having ignored at least one reasonably clear instance of cheating (Graham et al., 1994; Tabachnick et al., 1991). In addition, at institutions that require faculty members to report suspected cases of academic dishonesty, 70% to 80% of those who do take action ignore the reporting requirement and handle the incident themselves (Jendrek, 1989; McCabe, 1993; Singhal, 1982). As we discuss in chapters 4 and 5, such flouting of institutional policies is always the wrong thing to do. In this section, we discuss two causes of faculty members' reluctance to take action: denial that academic dishonesty is a problem and factors that inhibit faculty action.

Denial of the Problem

Although there are no empirical data on the issue, anecdotal evidence and some published opinion statements suggest that many faculty members deny the existence of, or necessity of dealing with, academic dishonesty.

TABLE 1.2
Academic Dishonesty Rates Found in McCabe and Trevino's (1993) Survey

Variable	All Institutions	Honor Code Institutions	Other Institutions
Committed any of the 12 behaviors	78.3%	57.8%	81.8%
Cheated on examinations	52.2%	30.9%	60.4%
Copied homework assignments	41.6%	25.3%	49.8%
Plagiarized	48.4%	31.0%	57.1%

Note. Calculated from data provided by Donald McCabe.

This denial seems to take three forms: (a) "Cheating doesn't happen in my classes," (b) "Cheating happens, but I'd rather not know about it," and (c) "Cheating happens, but it can promote learning."

"Cheating Doesn't Happen in My Classes." Given the enormous body of data documenting the prevalence of academic dishonesty, it may seem odd that anyone could deny its existence. However, consider views such as this:

> In 53 years of teaching I have been violated by cheating students on less than a handful of occasions. I refuse to spend inordinate time and effort chasing the minuscule fraction of those who abuse themselves and their fellow students. Far better to serve those who seek to learn. (Saltman, 1996, p. 5)

Although we all wish to "serve those who seek to learn," Saltman's implication that such service is incompatible with the control of academic dishonesty is simply incorrect. In addition, by controlling cheating and other forms of academic dishonesty, we are serving learning-oriented students (e.g., Johnston, 1996). In chapter 3 we discuss a number of techniques that both enhance learning and are likely to promote academic integrity.

Students want their instructors to take action against cheaters. They view faculty members' refusal to confront it as unethical (Keith-Spiegel, Tabachnick, & Allen, 1993) and respond negatively to instructors who ignore the problem. Keith-Spiegel (1999), for example, had four groups of students rate how much they respected instructors who used one of four types of exam-monitoring styles. The least admired style was that of the lax instructor who kept his nose in his own work and occasionally left the room, paying no attention to the students taking the exam. When the students were asked to supply adjectives describing this instructor, *naive* and *dumb* were the most frequent. When asked how much cheating would go on during this exam, the ratings for the lax instructor far exceeded the estimates of the other styles, all of which involved various levels of vigilance.

"I Don't Want to Know About It." Other faculty members, imitating the ostrich of lore, prefer to keep their heads buried in the sand, avoiding the problem of academic dishonesty by making sure they do not see it. Consider one anonymous student's experience:

> "During one exam last month, I had the proctors standing right next to me talking to one another, saying how they were directed by the professor not to catch anybody cheating: 'If you see somebody cheating walk up from behind them, maybe they'll get scared and stop it. But it's a multiple choice exam and that's the sort of cheating that's too hard to prove, so don't even do it. Don't bother!'" (Connell, 1981, p. 27)

An attitude such as this one does not prevent cheating, but encourages it (Genereaux & McLeod, 1995). The student just quoted described the cheating in the class by saying, "the whole place was like a circus" (Connell, 1981, p. 27). Although it can be difficult to detect student cheating (as we discuss in chap. 4), there are a number of effective techniques for preventing it even on multiple-choice exams.

"Cheating Is Really a Form of Learning." A third form of denial rationalizes dishonesty away as simply another mode of learning. K. Davis (1992) wrote of how he briefly left his classroom during an exam. On looking in the window before returning, he saw several students discussing the test questions among themselves. However, Davis reasoned, this behavior was not a problem because people in the real world had to work collaboratively to solve problems:

> I realized I wasn't looking at cheaters; I was looking at collaborators. I wasn't looking at students copying answers; I was looking at students solving problems. I wasn't

looking at rapscallions sabotaging the educational system; I was looking at students preparing for successful lives in the real world. (K. Davis, 1992, p. 74)

Davis was apparently *not* looking at the students in the class who, following the rules that he had presumably set, were not collaborating but were working independently—students whose grades might have been undermined by the collaborators' actions. He was also apparently not looking at the message he was sending about how to succeed in the real world: Cheating for success is acceptable as long as you can get away with it. However, the real world no longer works that way or at least not as much as it used to: Many large corporations are instituting and enforcing corporate ethics programs; they want employees who succeed honestly (e.g., McCabe et al., 1996; Paine, 1994; Trevino, 1990).

Factors Inhibiting Faculty Action

Even those faculty members who see academic dishonesty as a problem and are willing to deal with it probably do so reluctantly: Keith-Spiegel et al. (1998) found that 77% of the college and university faculty members they surveyed agreed or strongly agreed with the statement, "Dealing with a cheating student is one of the most onerous aspects of the job." In this section we discuss some of the factors that make it difficult to deal with academic dishonesty.

Emotional Stress. Keith-Spiegel et al. (1998) found that the instructors in their sample rated the high degrees of anxiety and stress associated with accusing a student of academic dishonesty as the second most important reason why they thought instructors ignored cheating. (Insufficient evidence of cheating received the highest rating.) Carrying out unpleasant tasks is indeed stressful, and that stress is often compounded by a feeling of being let down by the student. However, there are some ways to cope with the stress; which we outline as part of our discussion of dealing with cheating in chapter 5.

Lack of Information and Training. Instructors generally have little information about how to deal effectively with academic dishonesty in terms of either prevention of dishonesty or the procedures to follow when faced with a case of suspected academic dishonesty. This lack of information both causes and compounds some of the stresses inherent in the process. For example, if you were to consult one of the growing number of handbooks on college and university teaching, you would find that the authors and editors of these handbooks provide surprisingly little information on the topic of academic dishonesty. We conducted an informal survey of recent how-to books on college teaching available in our university library. Of the six books published since 1991, three did not include the topic of cheating (although one included a set of chapters on "special problems that confront the undergraduate faculty member"). Each of the other three dedicated no more than five pages to the topic, and only one provided any specific advice on the nature of cheating, how to prevent and detect it, and how to deal with cheaters.

Another potential source of information is training programs at the colleges and universities in which instructors teach. However, like the authors of teaching handbooks, colleges and universities only rarely provide information on academic dishonesty. Kibler (1994) conducted a survey of 191 four-year public and private colleges and universities concerning their policies on academic integrity and dishonesty. He found that less than half of the responding institutions provided any sort of instructor training on the topics. Although the percentages of public and private institutions providing training did not differ, the content of the training did. Among the institutions that did provide training, private colleges and universities were about equally likely to provide training on strategies for preventing academic dishonesty and handling any instances that arise. However, private institutions were somewhat less likely to provide training on definitions of academic dishonesty and sanctions for academic dishonesty, and were much less likely to provide training on classroom and testing techniques that promote academic integrity. Some of these differences may have resulted from more of the private institutions having honor codes. Honor codes address most of the latter topics, which may have made discussion of them appear unnecessary. However, Kibler did not break his results down by the presence or absence of honor codes.

Kibler found that 94% of the responding public institutions and 84% of the responding private institutions reported providing case assistance or consultation for faculty dealing with instances of academic dishonesty. However, about 65% of each type of institution also reported having no office specifically tasked with the responsibility to coordinate efforts to reduce or control academic dishonesty. Hence, this advice and assistance may be hard to find at most institutions.

Time-Consuming Processes. Resolving cases of academic dishonesty can take a considerable amount of time. For example, collecting evidence of dishonesty—especially in cases of suspected plagiarism, in which the search for evidence may entail an arduous review of possible source material—can be a daunting prospect. Once evidence is found, resolving the case may require one or more hearings before an administrator or judicial board; in the end, the student may be exonerated despite an instructor's certainty that cheating occurred. The decision about whether to devote a large amount of time to documenting academic dishonesty may be especially difficult for newer faculty members. As Gary Pavela noted,

> If you're a young faculty member up for tenure and your campus has a complex and convoluted process which takes weeks and weeks to resolve a case, in which you are subject to intensive cross-examination by an attorney, and then the case is appealed internally within a university and drags on for a long period of time, you have to make a choice whether you want to get involved in that process or if you want to continue writing your article to get tenure. (Quoted by Connell, 1981, p. 23)

Although the search for evidence may be difficult and time-consuming, and although some hearing processes are unnecessarily cumbersome (Gehring & Pavela, 1994; Kibler et al., 1988), deciding to ignore cases of academic dishonesty also entails costs. Ignoring dishonesty gives the impression of condoning (or at least tolerating) it, and students who waver between acting honestly and dishonestly may decide that dishonesty is acceptable for this instructor (e.g., Genereaux & McLeod, 1995). In chapter 6 we discuss ways in which the institution can assist faculty in dealing with academic dishonesty in ways that ease the stress and time costs.

Impression Management. Hardy (1981) suggested that some instructors prefer to overlook academic dishonesty because they are concerned that reporting it would reflect negatively on their teaching abilities. New instructors, especially, might believe that department chairs and members of promotion and tenure committees might decide that student cheating indicates a lack of teaching ability or a failure to take action to prevent academic dishonesty. However, most faculty members are aware that academic dishonesty is a problem (e.g., Jendrek, 1989) and are likely to be sympathetic to a new instructor's plight. Consequently, veteran faculty members are more likely to offer advice and assistance than criticism to a less experienced colleague. In fact, most instructors view ignoring strong evidence of academic dishonesty as unethical (Morgan et al., 1996; Tabachnick et al., 1991) and so would probably have a more negative impression of a colleague who ignored academic dishonesty than one who pursued it to conclusion.

Impression management might also extend to students: Instructors might be concerned that pursuing a case of academic dishonesty could lead students to perceive them as too strict, which, in turn, could negatively affect teaching evaluations. However, and perhaps surprisingly given the prevalence of cheating, most students, like most instructors, perceive ignoring strong evidence of academic dishonesty to be unethical (Keith-Spiegel et al., 1993) and so would view an instructor who ignored a cheating peer more negatively than one who pursued it. Accused students might retaliate with poor teaching evaluations, but this problem could be dealt with administratively (see chapter 6).

Concern Over Litigation. In today's litigious society, concern over being sued appears to be reasonable, and students do sometimes sue over accusations of academic dishonesty. However, Gehring and Pavela (1994) noted that they

> have monitored and reviewed the pertinent case law related to academic integrity in higher education for over 30 years and have yet to find even one case in which administrators, faculty, or students have been assessed damages for reporting alleged acts of academic dishonesty. (p. 16)

These types of lawsuits have failed even when the students were exonerated of the accusation of dishonesty (Gehring & Pavela, 1994; Kibler et al., 1988). In addition, even if a faculty member is sued, most colleges and universities provide the faculty member with defense counsel because the faculty member's actions are part of his or her official duties (Gehring & Pavela, 1994).

There are only three conditions under which a faculty member is likely to be found liable for damages: (a) if the faculty member makes a knowingly false and malicious accusation, (b) if the faculty member violates the student's right to due process by ignoring the institution's procedures for resolving accusations of academic dishonesty, or (c) if the faculty member discusses the case using the student's name with individuals who are not involved in the process of resolving the matter (Gehring, 1998; Gehring & Pavela, 1994; Kibler et al., 1988). Therefore, a faculty member who makes an accusation of academic dishonesty in good faith, follows established procedures, and is discrete when discussing the case has little to fear in the way of legal liability. For those who still have residual concerns, many professional associations now offer professional liability insurance to college and university faculty members.

Fear of being sued is not the only nightmare scenario that faculty members could face. Without the support of the department chair or dean, one is alone and vulnerable. Stories circulate about instructors who, on presenting solid evidence of honesty policy violations to their administrative superiors, are ignored or left to face any fallout alone (e.g., Schneider, 1999). Without backing, it becomes understandable that some instructors in some institutions do not report academic dishonesty and may even disregard acts of academic dishonesty altogether. A second, probably less well-founded fear, that may cause some faculty members to avoid taking action is that an accused student may retaliate violently against the accuser. Although such incidents are rare, those such as one in which a law student attempted to hire someone to kill the secretary who apparently observed the student cheating do send a chilling message ("Law Student Arrested," 1995).

A Cautionary Note. Although we encourage instructors to confront the problem of academic dishonesty and deal with it proactively, it is important to bear in mind the rights students have when accused of dishonesty. For example, it would never be proper to bully a student into an admission of dishonesty no matter how certain one is of the student's guilt. We offer suggestions for handling these situations in chapters 4 and 5.

SUMMARY

In this chapter we pointed out the endemic nature of academic dishonesty among American college and university students. Although academic integrity should be a primary concern of faculty and administrators, they are often reluctant to take action on the problem. We showed how this reluctance can stem from denial that the problem exists and a variety of pragmatic concerns. In the next chapter we discuss the nature of academic dishonesty, describe student and faculty opinions on what constitutes academic dishonesty, and present a model of the causes of academic dishonesty.

2

Academic Dishonesty: What Is It and Why Do Students Engage in It?

◆ ◆ ◆

As shown in chapter 1, academic dishonesty is a pervasive problem that can have invidious effects on higher education and, therefore, should be of concern to all college and university students, teachers, and administrators. In this chapter we discuss the nature of academic dishonesty and its definitions, reasons students give for cheating, institutional and student characteristics associated with cheating, and the extent to which cheating actually leads to higher grades.

WHAT BEHAVIORS CONSTITUTE ACADEMIC DISHONESTY?

Academic dishonesty appears to be one of those phenomena that few people can define exactly, but that everyone can recognize when they see it. As Kibler (1993a) noted, "One of the most significant problems a review of the research on academic dishonesty reveals is the absence of a generally accepted definition" (p. 253). In this section we present a typology of academic dishonesty, examine faculty members' and students' views of what behaviors are and are not dishonest, and briefly consider the issue of possible cultural differences in definitions of *cheating* and *plagiarism*.

A Typology of Academic Dishonesty

One of the more widely cited definitions of *academic dishonesty* is that devised by Pavela (1978), who proposed a typology consisting of four components:

- *Cheating* is "intentionally using or attempting to use unauthorized materials, information, or study aids in any academic exercise. The term *academic exercise* includes all forms of work submitted for credit or hours" (p. 78). Thus, cheating includes such behaviors as using crib notes or copying during tests and unauthorized collaboration on out-of-class assignments.

- *Fabrication* is "intentional and unauthorized falsification or invention of any information or citation in an academic exercise" (p. 78). Thus, fabrication includes behaviors such as making up sources for the bibliography of a paper or faking the results of a laboratory experiment.

- *Plagiarism* is "deliberate adoption or reproduction of ideas or words or statements of another person as one's own without acknowledgement" (p. 78). Thus, plagiarism includes behaviors such as turning in a paper written by another student or buying a paper from a commercial source and failing to properly attribute quotations within a paper. Depending on institutional policy, it could also include what might be called *self-plagiarism*: submitting the same paper for credit in more than one course without the instructor's permission.

- *Facilitating academic dishonesty* is "intentionally or knowingly helping or attempting to help another" engage in some form of academic dishonesty (p. 78).

Although Pavela's (1978) typology encompasses a wide variety of behaviors, others could be added:

- *Misrepresentation* consists of providing false information to an instructor concerning an academic exercise (Hollinger & Lanza-Kaduce, 1996). Misrepresentation includes behaviors such as giving a false excuse for missing a test or deadline or falsely claiming to have submitted a paper.

- *Failure to contribute to a collaborative project* involves not doing one's fair share.

- *Sabotage* consists of actions that prevent others from completing their work (Stern & Havlicek, 1986). For example, disturbing someone's lab experiment or removing materials from a reserved reading file so that others cannot use them would be an act of academic sabotage.

Behaviors Faculty and Students View as Dishonest

A number of studies have been conducted to determine which behaviors faculty members and students consider to constitute academic dishonesty. The appendix to this chapter lists behaviors commonly considerd to be instances of academic dishonesty and summarizes student and faculty perceptions of the degree of dishonesty of the behaviors. The behaviors are organized by category of behavior (cheating, plagiarism, etc.), and categories have been subdivided into examination behaviors, behaviors relevant to out-of-class assignments, and behaviors relevant to laboratory work.

Students' Beliefs. Although research on what behaviors students see as being academically dishonest has generated a considerable amount of data, some generalizations are possible. Five norms appear to lead a substantial number of students not to view a behavior as dishonest:

1. *Tests already given are fair game as long as they are not stolen.* Students are tolerant of studying from old tests without the instructor's permission, getting test questions or answers from students in an earlier testing session, and memorizing test questions to add them to a test file.
2. *Taking shortcuts is okay.* Students are tolerant of reading a condensed version of an assigned work, reading a foreign language assignment in translation, listing unread sources in a paper's bibliography, and faking and fudging laboratory reports.
3. *Unauthorized collaboration with others is okay.* Students are tolerant of allowing someone to help with homework, copying homework, having someone check a paper for spelling or grammar when those elements are graded, and looking at someone else's test paper and keeping one's answer if the answer is the same. It is also noteworthy that, although most students defined most of the facilitation behaviors as dishonest, many also believe that such behaviors are justified when helping a friend. For example, McCabe (1992) found that 26% percent of the students who indicated that they had helped someone cheat had never themselves cheated. Similarly, students are more tolerant of someone who helps a friend cheat than they are of the cheater (Whitley & Kost, 1999; Wryobeck & Whitley, 1999).
4. *Some forms of plagiarism are okay.* Students are tolerant of omitting some sources used in a paper from the bibliography and of using direct quotations without citing the source.
5. *Conning teachers is okay.* Students are tolerant of giving false excuses for missing tests and deadlines and marking more than one response on a multiple-choice test in the hope that the instructor will assume that the correct answer was the intended one.

Faculty Members' Beliefs. Compared with students, faculty members view more behaviors as dishonest. Nonetheless, there are some behaviors that a substantial minority of faculty members do not consider to be cheating. These behaviors fall into four general categories:

1. *Behaviors that could be accidental,* such as marking more than one response on a multiple-choice question and not citing all the sources used in a paper in its bibliography.
2. *Behaviors that could be due to ignorance of proper behavior,* such as using a direct quote without citing the source.
3. *Behaviors that could be due to uncertainty over what is allowed,* such as having someone check a paper for spelling and grammatical errors when those elements are graded.
4. *Behaviors that approximate proper behavior,* such as reading a condensed version of a work rather than the complete version that was assigned.

Comparing Faculty Members' and Students' Views. Research comparing faculty and student attitudes bears out what we just saw: Although there are many areas of agreement, students generally view academic dishonesty more leniently than do faculty members (e.g., Barnett & Dalton, 1981; Graham et al., 1994; Roig & Ballew, 1994). However, faculty members tend to overestimate students' leniency. In contrast, students make accurate estimates of faculty members' attitudes (Barnett & Dalton, 1981; Graham et al., 1994; Roig & Ballew, 1994). In addition, students' attitudes tend to move closer to faculty members' attitudes as they move through college from their first year to their senior year (Sims, 1995). Therefore, faculty members may perceive more experienced students to be more lenient on academic dishonesty than they really are. One attitude that faculty members and students both hold is that intentional dishonesty, such as conspiring with another student to copy from one another on a test, is a more severe ethical violation than opportunistic dishonesty, such as looking at a test paper that another student leaves exposed when the opportunity unexpectedly arises (Livosky & Tauber, 1994).

Clearly differences in perceptions about what behaviors constitute cheating can cause problems, such as an instructor's believing that a student had cheated when the student sees nothing wrong with his or her behavior. Also, differences between instructors can cause confusion for students when one instructor is indifferent to a particular behavior, such as collaboration on homework, while another assumes (but does not explicitly state) that students will work independently on such assignments. As we discuss in the next chapter, one way to prevent these kinds of problems is to state explicitly what behaviors are and are not allowed for each type of assignment. Also, in chapter 6 we outline some prevention measures that can be taken at the institutional level.

Are There Cultural Differences in the Definition of Academic Dishonesty?

As American society grows more diverse and as America's colleges and universities increasingly reflect this diversity, the issue arises of the possibility of cultural differences in the definition of *academic dishonesty*. Professors who teach students who grew up outside the Euro-American cultural milieu may certainly face this problem on occasion. For example, Cordeiro (1995) related the experiences of some faculty members at a university he called Uni who noticed students from a country he called Jaxar engaging in behaviors that the faculty defined as *cheating* and *plagiarism*. When questioned about their behavior, the Jaxar students acknowledged their participation in the behaviors. However, they disagreed that their activities should be classified as cheating:

> The defense or rationale of the students . . . was that [their] behavior was accepted in Jaxar. . . . They viewed the behavior as "helping each other—as required by their culture." As explained by everyone from Jaxar, each person was viewed as a "brother" in an extended family. . . . Each "brother" was expected to assist other brothers, especially those who needed help in understanding the course material or in passing the exams. . . . What the University viewed as unethical cheating, the Jaxar students viewed as normal, perhaps even required, behavior. (p. 28; see also Robinson, 1992)

The concept of *plagiarism* might also be a difficult one for some international students. Not only is the notion that words or ideas belong to or owned by a person one that has developed relatively recently (see Box 2.1), it is also uniquely Western. Consequently, "students from certain Middle Eastern, Asian, and African cultures are baffled by the notion that one can 'own' ideas, since their cultures regard words and ideas as the property of all rather than as individual property" (McLeod, 1992, p. 12). As a result of this view of the communal nature of knowledge, students from these cultures see nothing wrong with using others' words and ideas without citing sources. Some of these students may even have been rewarded in the past for what the Western intellectual tradition considers to be plagiarism: "Chinese students . . . may repeat . . . verbatim something previously read . . . in the belief that this is a widely approved way to attain a high mark" (Hu & Grove, 1991, p. 83). Even the concept of paraphrasing

BOX 2.1
A Brief History of the Concept of Plagiarism

As academics, we are so familiar with these conventions [of citing and documenting sources] that we may forget how strange they actually are. The very notion of being able to "own" words or ideas is after all a relatively recent one. Classical notions of art involved mimesis, or imitation: originality was not valued, nor was the individual artist; writers borrowed freely from one another. Few of Shakespeare's plots were his own. A book of scholarship on one of Shakespeare's contemporaries is entitled euphemistically *John Webster's Borrowings;* Webster's plays are in fact a patchwork of quotations from other sources. It is perhaps not by accident that our modern notion of plagiarism was born at about the same time as two other ideas: the romantic notion of a single, original author expressing his innermost feelings through art, and the capitalist notion of private property. Ideas, words, and phrases are now (in what is surely a curious phrase) "intellectual property," to be trespassed upon only with permission of the owner. (McLeod, 1992, p. 12).

may be alien to some international students: "Some cultures feel it disrespectful to the author to alter the original words [of a source document]" (Robinson, 1992, p. 15).

The American emphasis on originality in academic work can also cause problems for students from cultures in which the emphasis is on self-effacement as well as learning and adhering to the ideas found in accepted authoritative works (Deckert, 1993; Robinson, 1992). These students might feel it necessary to disguise their ideas as those of experts in the field. In the words of one student,

> I remember in China I had even committed what I call "reversed plagiarism"—here, I suppose, it would be called "forgery"—when I was in middle school: willfully attributing some of my thoughts to "experts" when I needed some arguments but could not find a suitable quotation from a literary or political "giant." (Shen, 1989, p. 460)

As Cordeiro (1995) noted, problems such as these can be avoided by ensuring that all students are informed about what constitutes proper and improper academic behavior. In fact, the Uni administration did not accept the Jaxar students' explanation because the university's code of conduct explicitly defined cheating and plagiarism. (See chapt. 6 for ways to inform students about institutional integrity policies.) In addition, instructors can consult staff members at their institution's international student office for advice concerning the academic norms of specific cultures.

What about America's varied ethnic groups? Little research has been conducted on the existence of ethnic group difference in the definition of academic dishonesty, but what research has been done suggests that no differences exist. In a study of sixth, seventh, and eight graders, Anderman, Griesinger, and Westerfeld (1998) found no difference in self-reported cheating rates between African-American and White students, and neither Roig and Ballew (1994) nor Sutton and Huba (1995) found differences between African-American and White students' attitudes toward academic dishonesty. In addition, Roig and Ballew found no differences between the attitudes of members of those groups and the attitudes of Hispanic students. There appears to be no research that has included members of other ethnic groups.

WHY DO STUDENTS ENGAGE IN ACADEMIC DISHONESTY?

The answer to the question of why students engage in academic dishonesty may be obvious: to get a higher grade than they otherwise would. The question of why students behave dishonestly rather than doing the work honestly can, however, provide some insight into issues discussed later in this book, such as fostering academic integrity in the classroom and controlling academic dishonesty. Therefore, this section reviews the reasons that students give for engaging in and avoiding academic dishonesty and some additional factors that may influence students' behavior.

Students' Explanations for Their Behavior

Why Do Some Students Cheat? A fairly large number of studies have investigated the explanations students give for engaging in academic dishonesty. Table 2.1 summarizes these explanations and groups them into three broad categories: factors motivating academic dishonesty, reasons for engaging in academic dishonesty, and justifications for academic dishonesty.

As one would expect, one set of motivations for academic dishonesty centers around concern for performance in terms of both avoiding failure and getting a higher grade. Another set of motivations deals with pressures

TABLE 2.1
Reasons and Justifications Students Give for Academic Dishonesty

Factors Motivating Academic Dishonesty

Performance Concerns
  I will fail course without cheating.
  I want a better grade.
  I want to avoid flunking out of school.
  I need to pass course to graduate.
External Pressures
  Academic
    The work load across all courses is too heavy.
    Others' cheating puts me at a disadvantage.
    The professor [or readings] did not adequately explain material.
    There were too many tests on one day.
  Nonacademic
    My parents put pressure on me.
    My job leaves too little time to study.
    Illness prevented adequate preparation.
    My financial aid depends on my grade point average.
    I need good grades for job/graduate or professional school.
Unfair Professors
  Grading is too harsh.
  Tests are unfair and designed to fail students.
  My course work load is unreasonable.
Lack of Effort
  I did not attend class.
  I did not want to do the work.
Adherence to Other Loyalties
  I was helping a friend.
  I have loyalty to my group (e.g., fraternity or sorority).
Other
  An irresistible opportunity unexpectedly arose.
  Cheating is a game/challenge.

Reasons for Engaging in Academic Dishonesty

Few people ever get caught.
Academic dishonesty is not punished.
Other students don't cover their papers during tests.
The instructor left the room during the test.

TABLE 2.1 (continued)

Justifications for Academic Dishonesty

> Denial of Injury
>> Cheating hurts no one.
>> Cheating is only wrong in courses in your major.
>
> Denial of Personal Responsibility
>> I got the flu and couldn't read all of the chapters.
>> The class is too hard.
>> Professors don't care about students.
>
> Denial of Personal Risk
>> Professors won't do anything to you.
>> No one ever gets caught.
>
> Selective Morality
>> I only cheat to get through tough classes.
>> I am an honest person, but I did what was necessary at the time.
>> Friends come first, and she needed my help.
>
> Minimizing Seriousness
>> Cheating is meaningless when assignment has little weight in final grade.
>> It's only busy work.
>
> A Necessary Act
>> If I don't do well in college, my parents will kill me.
>> I could lose my scholarship if I don't get all Bs.
>
> Dishonesty as a Norm
>> Society's leaders do it, so why not me?
>> Everyone does it.
>> Professors and administrators tolerate cheating.

Note. Data are from Aiken (1991), Brown (1995), Davis, Grover, Becker, and McGregor (1992), Davis and Ludvigson (1995), Diekhoff et al. (1996), Faulkender et al. (1994), Franklyn-Stokes and Newstead (1995), Genereaux and McLeod (1995), Graham et al. (1994), LaBeff, Clark, Haines, and Diekhoff (1990), McCabe (1992), McCabe et al. (1999), Nuss (1984), and Sutton and Huba (1995).

that students claim to be under, some of which may be real and others of which may be rationalizations for dishonesty, but all of which shift the responsibility for their behavior away from themselves. Academic pressures include work overloads, improper explanation of the material, and cheating as a defense against others' cheating. Nonacademic pressures include parental demands for high grades, performance requirements for financial aid, lack of time to study due to a job or illness, and wanting high grades to impress employers or graduate and professional schools. Some students claim that cheating is a means of "balancing the books," as it were, with professors whom they perceive to be acting unfairly, such as requiring too heavy a work load, giving tests that are too difficult, and grading too harshly.

Some students admit to a lack of effort—not attending class, not wanting to do the work—as a reason for their academic dishonesty. Other students claim that, as it were, "the devil made me do it": They say they gave into an irresistible temptation when an opportunity to cheat arose. Still others see cheating as a game or contest of wits between themselves and their professors. Finally, students say that facilitation of academic dishonesty is motivated by adherence to loyalties outside the academic domain, such as the duties of friendship or those owed to fellow members of one's fraternity or sorority.

Students also provide reasons why they proceed to actually engage in academic dishonesty once they are motivated to do so. These facilitating factors include the perception that few people get caught or that academic dishonesty is not punished. Students say that cheating on exams is facilitated by other students not covering their papers and the instructor leaving the room. Like the claims of external pressures, these latter reasons allow students to blame someone else for their own behavior.

Finally, students claim that their dishonest behavior can be justified on a number of grounds. One justification is that academic dishonesty is permissible because, even if it is a crime, it is victimless because it hurts no one. Another justification is that a specific act of dishonesty is trivial because it does not affect one's grade in an important assignment or course. Some students claim that academic dishonesty is justifiable on the grounds that professors do not care about students, so why should students care about what is important to professors? Finally, students may see academic dishonesty as justified because society's leaders model unethical behavior, academic dishonesty is the norm at their institution, or faculty members and administrators tolerate it.

Although many of these reasons and justifications may be self-serving, fallacious, or based on misperceptions, it is important to remember that whether students' beliefs are true is irrelevant to their behavior. It is the fact that they hold these beliefs, or see them as reasonable justifications for dishonesty, that affects their behavior.

Why Do Some Students Not Cheat? Although fewer studies have investigated students' reasons for not engaging in academic dishonesty than have investigated their explanations for engaging in academic dishonesty, such explanations are nonetheless informative. Table 2.2 summarizes these explanations and groups them into two broad categories: internal reasons relating to students' attitudes, beliefs, and value system; and external factors relating to situational constraints on dishonesty.

Clearly, some students avoid academic dishonesty because of their ethical objections to it in contrast to those students who believe that dishonesty is justified under at least some circumstances. Similarly, in contrast to those students who engage in academic dishonesty because of concerns over performance, there are those who eschew academic dishonesty because they are confident of their abilities or see cheating as rendering success meaningless. However, some students say that they have not engaged in academic dishonesty because they never thought of it or did not think they had the skill to get away with it.

Many external constraints on academic dishonesty are mirror images of some students' reasons for the behavior. In contrast to those students who engage in academic dishonesty because of the perceived low probability of being caught or punished, others avoid it because they believe they are likely to be discovered and perceive a high cost for being caught. In contrast to students who justify dishonesty as normative, others avoid it because their friends disapprove or because the teacher would lose respect from them. Finally, in contrast to those who see academic dishonesty as victimless, other avoid it because they view it as unfair to other students. (Creating a "Campus Ethos" that values integrity is discussed in chapt. 6.)

Other Factors Influencing Academic Dishonesty

When we think of academic dishonesty, we usually focus on instances of intentional dishonesty: The student knows that a behavior is prohibited but nonetheless carries it out, using one of the reasons discussed earlier to justify the behavior. However, some students may unintentionally engage in what faculty members consider to be academically dishonest behaviors for two reasons: They do not know that the behavior is prohibited or, as is often found in cases of plagiarism, they know the behavior is prohibited but don't have the skills necessary to avoid it.

Lack of Understanding of What Is Prohibited. As we saw in the discussion of definitions of academic dishonesty, students do not always agree with faculty members on the behaviors that constitute academic dishonesty. This disagreement may be aggravated in situations in which the status of

TABLE 2.2
Reasons Students Give for *Not* Engaging in Academic Dishonesty

Internal Reasons

> Believe that it is wrong
> It makes success meaningless
> Too proud to do it
> Can succeed without it
> Never thought of it
> Don't know how to do it without getting caught
> Respect for the teacher

External Reasons

> High cost of getting caught
> High likelihood of getting caught
> Embarrassment over getting caught
> Teacher would lose respect for me
> Friends disapprove
> It's unfair to other students

Note. Data are from Diekhoff et al. (1996), Franklyn-Stokes and Newstead (1995), Graham et al. (1994), and Hendershott, Drinan, and Cross (1999).

the behavior is ambiguous. For example, a faculty member may intend that students work independently on an assignment and assume the students know that independent work is required, and therefore not specifically tell them not to collaborate. Consequently, students accused of unauthorized collaboration on the assignment could, with real justification, protest that "You never said we couldn't work on it together." After all, some instructors allow or encourage collaboration on some assignments.

Because some students might not understand what behaviors are prohibited, Roth and McCabe (1995) emphasized the importance of student–faculty agreement on the behaviors that comprise academic dishonesty. For example, they found that students whose views of what constituted cheating on exams coincided with their university's definition of cheating were much less likely to report having cheated on exams than were students whose views did not coincide with the university's definition. Therefore, establishing clear rules that define authorized and prohibited behaviors, especially in ambiguous situations such as student collaboration, can prevent the occurrence of at least some cases of academic dishonesty.

Inability to Avoid Prohibited Behaviors. Even when students understand that a behavior is prohibited, they may lack the skills that will allow them to avoid it. This situation is especially common in cases of plagiarism. For example, Roig (1997), found that even when students understand the concept of plagiarism, they often cannot recognize it when presented with examples. Roig gave students a copy of a paragraph from a research report, along with several other versions of the paragraph, two of which consisted of proper paraphrases of the original. The other versions represented various degrees of plagiarism, including lack of citation of the source and occasional substitution of synonyms for the original phrasing. Roig found that, averaged across all the examples of plagiarism, fewer than half the students could correctly identify the plagiarized paragraphs. He concluded that, from the average student's point of view, "as long as the original author is credited and/or as long as minor modifications are made to the original, the material is generally considered to be properly paraphrased." Consequently, "a substantial amount of [plagiarism] may stem from ignorance, on the part of students, over the proper rules for correctly paraphrasing text" (Roig, 1997, p. 121).

STUDENT AND INSTITUTIONAL CHARACTERISTICS ASSOCIATED WITH ACADEMIC DISHONESTY

Considerable research has been conducted on factors associated with academic dishonesty, especially cheating. The factors studied have included demographic, personality, and behavioral characteristics of students; institutional characteristics; and control measures, such as proctoring during exams. Because Bushway and Nash (1977), Cizek (1999), and Whitley (1998) have extensively reviewed this literature, we only summarize it briefly. In this section, we will discuss student and institutional characteristics associated with academic dishonesty; control measures are discussed in chapter 4.

Student Characteristics

Whitley (1998) reviewed the research literature on factors associated with academic dishonesty published from 1975 to 1996. Table 2.3 summarizes his findings on student characteristics. We have organized the characteristics into six categories—demographic characteristics, academic characteristics, beliefs and perceptions, personality characteristics, and behavioral characteristics—and have categorized the strength of each characteristic's relationship with academic dishonesty as strong, moderate, small, or none.

As you can see from Table 2.3, few factors are *strongly* associated with academic dishonesty, perhaps reflecting the strong influence that control measures can have in preventing its occurrence. In addition, most of the factors that are strongly related to academic dishonesty are beliefs, perceptions, and behavioral patterns. Because instructors rarely have the opportunity to directly observe these factors, they are of limited value in identifying potential violators. However, there are several factors that may be useful in identifying students who are at risk for dishonesty: those who are younger, those who perform less well in the course but do have some expectation of success, and those with high workloads.

Also of interest is the finding that academic dishonesty is not an isolated characteristic of cheaters. Students who cheat show a pattern of involvement in other forms of minor deviance such as risky driving behaviors, lying to friends, negative on-the-job behaviors, and bullying (Berthold & Hoover, 2000; Blankenship & Whitley, 2000).

Interestingly, the research indicates that some factors stereotypically associated with academic dishonesty are actually small or nonexistent. For example, women cheat at about the same rate as men. Degree of religious belief was unrelated to amount of self-reported cheating. Although members of fraternities and sororities are slightly more likely to report having cheated than are nonmembers, they are no more likely to do so than other students heavily involved in extracurricular activities.

Institutional Characteristics

Research on institutional characteristics associated with student academic dishonesty is almost nonexistent. The only factor to receive attention has been the presence or absence of an honor code at the institution. Colleges and universities with honor codes are those in which students pledge to abide by a code that specifies appropriate and inappropriate academic behavior and in which students are responsible for administering and enforcing the code. As noted in chapter 1, in a survey of several thousand students enrolled at 31 institutions, McCabe and Trevino (1993) found that a smaller proportion of students at these colleges and universities

TABLE 2.3
Characteristics of Students Admitting to Academic Dishonesty

Type of Characteristic	Degree of Relationship
Demographic	
Are younger	Moderate
Are unmarried	Moderate
Are financially supported by their parents	Small
Live away from their parents	Small
Year in college	None
Parents' level of education	None
Sex of student	None
Academic	
Perform less well in the course	Moderate
Report having high academic workloads	Moderate
Are faced with important outcomes	Moderate
Have lower grade point averages	Small
Educational goals	None
Academic aptitude	None
Beliefs and Perceptions	
Have moderate expectations for success	Strong
Hold favorable attitudes toward academic dishonesty	Strong
Perceive that social norms allow dishonesty	Strong
Anticipate high reward for success	Strong
Report feeling pressure to get high grades	Moderate
Feel little moral obligation not to cheat	Moderate
Perceive greater competition for grades	Moderate
Perceive a high benefit-to-risk ratio for dishonest behavior	Moderate
Expect less punishment if caught	Small
See the instructor as unfair	Small
Personality	
Are more grade oriented and less learning oriented	Small
Have higher achievement motivation	Small
Are less industrious	Small
Are more alienated from academic and social values	Small
Experience higher test anxiety	Small
Have a higher need for approval	Small
Degree of religious belief	None
Self-esteem	None
Fear of being evaluated negatively	None

TABLE 2.3 (continued)

Type of Characteristic	Degree of Relationship
Behavioral	
Have cheated in the past	Strong
Party more frequently	Strong
Show a generally pattern of mildly deviant behavior	Moderate
Miss class often	Small
Are more involved in extracurricular activities	Small
Are members of fraternities or sororities	Small
Procrastinate more	Small
Time spent studying	None

Note. Adapted from Whitley (1998), Table 6. A variable with a strong relationship has a correlation greater than .50 with academic dishonesty, a variable with a moderate relationship has a correlation between .30 and .49, and a variable with a small relationship has a correlation between .10 and .29 (Cohen, 1992).

report engaging in academic dishonesty than at institutions without honor codes (see Table 1.2). Although these differences might be attributed to smaller enrollments or more selectivity in admitting students among honor code schools, McCabe and Trevino matched schools on these factors and so eliminated them as possible causes of the difference. Similarly, McCabe et al. (1999) found that students at honor code and non-honor-code schools reported experiencing the same academic pressures students cite as justifications for academic dishonesty (Table 2.1). Hence, the campus culture associated with an honor code makes a contribution to academic dishonesty.

However, the simple establishment of an honor code is not sufficient to reduce academic dishonesty; rather, the honor code reflects the presence of a normative climate that frowns on dishonesty. For example, Sierles, Kushner, and Krause (1988) examined the effect of the presence or absence of proctors on self-reported cheating on medical school examinations after the school had adopted an honor code. They found more self-reported cheating on the unproctored examinations. Thus, as McCabe and Trevino (1993) noted, the establishment of an honor code is probably not sufficient to deter academic dishonesty without a change in student norms regarding dishonesty. We discuss some strategies for developing an institutional culture of integrity in chapter 6.

A THEORETICAL MODEL OF
ACADEMIC DISHONESTY

Based on his literature review, Whitley (1998) organized the variables that he found to be related to academic dishonesty into a tentative causal model of academic dishonesty. For ease of presentation, we have divided the model into two parts, with proposed proximal causes of cheating shown in Figure 2.1 and proposed causes of one of the proposed distal causes shown in Figure 2.2.

Figure 2.1 illustrates the proposed proximal potential causes of cheating. Following the process postulated by the theory of planned behavior (Ajzen, 1991), the model holds that academically dishonest behavior is based on an intention to perform the behavior. However, the extent to which that intention actually results in behavior is affected by the extent to which the situation constrains the behavior. Examples of such situational constraints in an exam situation (discussed in more detail in chap. 4) would be close proctoring (which increases the risk of detection), increased physical distance between students, and the use of alternate forms of the test. Academic dishonesty would be less likely in high-constraint situations even if an intention to perform a dishonest behavior exists.

The model holds that the intention to engage in academic dishonesty is based on three factors: (a) attitudes toward academic dishonesty, including perceived norms concerning academic dishonesty and moral obligations not to engage in academic dishonesty (from the theory of planned behavior); (b) benefits expected to accrue from academic dishonesty; and (c) perceived risk of being caught.

A positive risk–benefit analysis accompanied by a positive attitude toward academic dishonesty, perception of a normative structure that allows academic dishonesty, and lack of a felt moral obligation to avoid academic dishonesty lead to the formation of an intention to perform a dishonest behavior. The model does not address whether these factors combine additively to contribute to an intention to engage in academic dishonesty or whether the variables interact with one another because the existing research literature has not addressed that question. An interactive

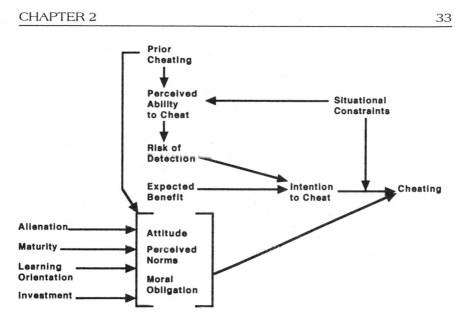

FIG. 2.1. Model of the proximate causes of academic dishonesty.

Adapted from Bernard E. Whitley, Jr. (1998). Factors Associated with Cheating Among College Students: A Review. *Research in Higher Education*, vol. 39, no. 3, pp. 235-274. Adapted with permission.

hypothesis might be that a negative attitude toward academic dishonesty inhibits dishonesty when the benefit-to-risk ratio is either high or low, but that a positive attitude facilitates dishonesty only when the benefit-to-risk ratio exceeds a certain threshold.

Risk of detection is a function of one's perceived ability to perform the intended behavior successfully, which is derived from prior experience and one's expectations of the constraints to be found in the situation. The attitudinal variables derive from a number of sources. Alienation, a generally deviant behavior pattern, and prior success at academic dishonesty make attitudes more positive, lead to a perception that norms support academic dishonesty, and lessen feelings of moral obligation to avoid academic dishonesty. Variables such as a learning orientation toward college and variables classified by Diekhoff et al. (1996) as maturity (such as age, being married, being self-supporting) and investment in education (such as working to pay for college) have the opposite effect.

Figure 2.2 illustrates the proposed antecedents of the expected benefit of academic dishonesty, which include the perceived importance of success, expected level of performance, and need for approval. The importance of success is a function of the expected reward value of success, perceived

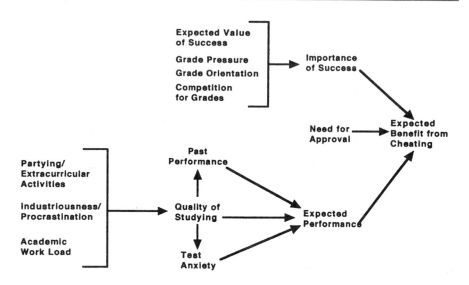

FIG. 2.2. Proposed model of causes of expected benefits of academic dishonesty.

Adapted from Bernard E. Whitley, Jr. (1998). Factors Associated with Cheating Among College Students: A Review. *Research in Higher Education*, vol. 39, no. 3, pp. 235-274. Adapted with permission.

grade pressure, grade orientation, and high competition for grades. As Houston (1978) found, uncertainty about whether one will succeed or fail increases the perceived benefit of academic dishonesty. Performance expectations are based on past performance, quality of one's study habits, and, for examinations, test anxiety. The quality of study is probably positively related to industriousness and inversely related to factors such as partying, involvement in extracurricular activities, procrastination, and academic workload. Need for approval contributes to the expected benefit of academic dishonesty to the extent that the student expects to receive approval from important others for success and disapproval for failure.

This model is, of necessity, somewhat tentative because the research literature has not comprehensively addressed all the relationships it proposes. However, it does help organize the research findings on the topic of academic dishonesty. We use it in chapters 3 and 4 when we discuss techniques for fostering academic integrity and measures for controlling academic dishonesty.

HOW DOES ACADEMIC DISHONESTY AFFECT
STUDENT PERFORMANCE?

As we noted earlier, obtaining higher grades is one of the reasons students cheat. Not only do students give this as a reason for academic dishonesty, but they also believe that academic dishonesty is an effective means to that end. In a survey of over 2,000 undergraduate students, Davis, Noble, Zak, and Dreyer (1994) found that 87% of their male respondents and 54% of their female respondents answered "yes" when asked "Does cheating improve exam scores?" Yet, does cheating actually improve test performance? Research suggests that the answer is "no," at least in the context of the only behavior studied so far—cheating on tests.

The first studies to address this question appear to be a pair of laboratory experiments conducted by Houston (Houston, 1977; Houston & Ziff, 1976). In one condition, the answer key to a memory test was purposely left exposed. Houston found that students who had the opportunity to copy answers from the "carelessly left exposed" answer key performed less well than students who had no such opportunity, suggesting that cheating may actually impair test performance. The results of field research also suggest that cheating is not effective in improving test performance. Hindman (1980) and Tigwell (1987) reported no effect on exam performance when students were allowed to bring notes written on 3 x 5- or 6 x 8-inch cards to exams, and Whitley (1996) found no effect when he allowed students to take exams aided by an 8.5 x 11-inch page written with notes on both sides.

These results seem counterintuitive, but they are explainable in the context of a timed test. Some students may use the notes as a substitute for studying, but during the test find they cannot look up all the answers and complete the test within the time allocated. Therefore, they lose points by omitting or guessing on some items. As Houston (1977) concluded, "cheating may not be an efficient strategy for improving test performance and . . . an uncritical belief in the efficacy of cheating behavior may be misleading" (p. 368).

SUMMARY

In this chapter we discussed definitions of *academic dishonesty* and pointed out areas of agreement and disagreement between instructors and students and among instructors. We noted that some behaviors seen by American faculty members as dishonest may not be viewed that way by international students, whose cultures view those behaviors as proper. However, there seems to be little disagreement among members of U.S. cultural groups on what constitutes academic dishonesty.

Students cite a number of reasons for engaging in academic dishonesty, including performance concerns and external pressures, and justify their behavior with a number of rationales, including denying that the behavior is harmful and denigrating the value of the assignments on which they cheated. Students may also lack an understanding of what behaviors are prohibited and may lack the skills necessary to avoid some behaviors, such as plagiarism. Some of the characteristics that strongly distinguish between cheaters and noncheaters include having moderate (vs. high or low) expectations of success in a course, positive attitudes toward cheating, perception that the student culture supports cheating, expecting high rewards for success, and having successfully cheated in the past.

We concluded by presenting a theoretical model of academic dishonesty and noting that cheating is often not as useful as many students think. In the next chapter we discuss some strategies instructors can use to foster academic integrity in their classrooms.

APPENDIX 2.1: PROFESSORS' AND STUDENTS' RATINGS OF THE LEVELS OF ACADEMIC DISHONESTY OF VARIOUS BEHAVIORS

Because studies of perceptions of the dishonesty of various behaviors have used a variety of means to assess beliefs about the behaviors, we have summarized the results using a 5-point scale. A 5 indicates that at least 90% of the respondents believed that a behavior constituted academic dishonesty, a 4 indicates that 75% to 89% believed the behavior to be dishonest, a 3 indicates that 50% to 74% believed the behavior to be dishonest, a 2 indicates that 25% to 49% believed the behavior to be dishonest, and a 1 indicates that less than 25% believed the behavior to be dishonest. Behaviors on which faculty members and students show fairly large disagreement (2 or more points) are shown in boldface.

	Dishonesty Rating	
	Professors	*Students*
Cheating —Examinations		
Asking another student for an answer during an exam	5	5
Getting test answers from an old copy of the exam	5	5
Using crib notes during an exam	5	5
Asking someone to take an exam for you	5	5
Copying answers from another student during an exam	5	5
Arranging with another student to copy answers during an exam	5	5
Getting a copy of an exam by having a student who is not enrolled in the course sit in on an earlier exam session and steal a copy of the exam	5	5
Tearing out a page or pages from an exam and taking it with you when the teacher does not permit you to keep the exam	5	5

Intentionally looking at another student's answer and keeping your answer if it is the same	5	3
Studying from an old exam without the teacher's permission	5	3
Getting exam answers from someone who took the exam earlier	4	3
Cheating—Assignments Writing a paper in English and having someone else translate it into translate into the required foreign language	5	4
Unauthorized collaboration	4	2
Reading an assignment in English when it is assigned in a foreign language	4	2
Having a term paper corrected for errors in spelling, grammar, and so on when those elements are being graded	3	1
Plagiarism Copying someone else's term paper	5	5
Having someone write a term paper for you	5	5
Buying a term paper	5	5
Using information from another student's paper without citing it	5	3
Using a paper for more than one class without the teacher's permission	4	2
Not citing all sources used in a paper in the bibliography	4	2
Fabrication—Assignments Making up sources for a bibliography	5	4
Listing real but unread sources in a bibliography	4	3

Fabrication—Laboratory Work
**Changing data so they look better in a
lab report** 5 3

**Writing a lab report without doing the
experiment** 5 3

Facilitating Dishonesty—Examinations
Signaling answers during an exam 5 5

Taking an exam for someone else 5 5

Giving someone an answer during an exam 5 5

Allowing someone to copy during an exam 5 5

Giving exam questions to students who take
the exam later 5 5

Facilitation—Assignments
Writing a paper for someone else 5 5

Selling a term paper 5 4

Allowing someone to copy homework 4 2

Misrepresentation—General
Falsely claiming to have handed in an exam or
assignment 5 5

**Giving a false excuse for missing an exam or
deadline** 5 3

Misrepresentation—Examinations
Changing an answer after an exam was graded
and reporting it as a scoring error 5 5

Misrepresentation—Assignments
**Reading a condensed version of a novel, play,
and so on, rather than assigned full version** 3 1

Noncontribution to Group Work
Not doing fair share of group work 5 4

Sabotage
Removing items from a reserved reading file so
that others cannot use them   5   4

Note. Data are from Barnett and Dalton (1981), Graham et al. (1994), Livosky and Tauber (1994), Sims (1995), Stern and Havlicek (1986), and Tom and Borin (1988).

II

Applications

3

Fostering Academic Integrity in the Classroom

◆ ◆ ◆

In this part, we present a number of suggestions for fostering academic integrity and preventing, detecting, and dealing with academic dishonesty at the classroom level. We have gleaned these suggestions from a variety of sources in the scholarly literature and institutional policies and publications, making it impossible to cite every author who has discussed a specific technique. An example would be the suggestion to increase the space between students as a way to prevent students from copying on exams. Many of these suggestions have appeared so often and in so many forms that it seems reasonable to consider them as being in the public domain. Instead of trying to cite every mention of a technique, we have chosen to cite selectively, and we apologize to any author whom we do not cite who has written about a particular technique.

This chapter emphasizes the positive side of the issue by discussing ways in which instructors can foster academic integrity in their classrooms. Chapters 4 and 5 deal with the negative and more anxiety-producing aspects of handling academic dishonesty, such as preventing and detecting academic dishonesty and confronting suspected cheaters.

ESTABLISHING A SUPPORTIVE CLASSROOM CLIMATE

Classroom climate is a term that refers to the social-psychological context of student–teacher interactions usually defined in terms of the students' perceptions of the teacher (e.g., Rosenfeld, 1983). A classroom climate can be either positive, fostering the academic goals of the course by being warm, supportive, and instructing, or it can be negative, hindering attainment of those goals by being cold, uncaring, and punishing. A negative climate motivates students to retaliate against the teacher for his or her perceived lack of interest in them (and their education) by engaging in a variety of behaviors. These reactions include cheating, plagiarism, and lying to the teacher (Pulvers & Diekhoff, 1999). In contrast, a positive classroom climate helps students learn and increases their motivation, thus enhancing the rewards of teaching as well as encouraging academic integrity (Rosenfeld, 1983).

We doubt that many college and university instructors purposely set out to create negative classroom climates. However, because classroom climate results from students' *interpretations* of instructors' behavior rather than the *intent* of the behavior, many instructors may inadvertently create, if even only to a minor degree, the kind of classroom climate that can lead students to justify academic dishonesty to themselves. This section focuses on *perceived fairness*—the aspect of classroom climate that appears to be most closely related to academic dishonesty.

Fairness and Academic Dishonesty

We saw in chapter 2 that students often cite the perceived unfairness of their instructors as a motivation for academic dishonesty. Although you might be tempted to dismiss these reasons as after-the-fact rationalizations for academic dishonesty, as Whitley and Kite (1998) pointed out, the idea that academic dishonesty may stem in part from students' perceptions of unfairness is consistent with the principles of equity theory (e.g., Mowday, 1991). Psychologists developed equity theory to address the question of how people decide whether an outcome is fair and the ways in which people attempt to rectify instances of perceived unfairness. The theory views fairness in terms of a social exchange: The social and material rewards that people receive from an endeavor should be proportional to the resources and effort they put into it. Conversely, unfairness or inequity exists when one's rewards are disproportionate to one's inputs, as when one has to work extremely hard to get a small reward. Although the theory holds that both over- and underreward produce feelings of inequity, it is underreward that has been most studied, and it is in that sense that we use the term *inequity* here.

Inequity is an aversive state, so people are motivated to reduce it by reestablishing equity; that is, by making their inputs and outputs proportional. Equity theory proposes a number of mechanisms for reducing feelings of inequity, the most studied of which is reducing one's inputs to match one's rewards (Mowday, 1991). For example, workers who believe they are underpaid often reduce their productivity to a level they feel is consistent with the rewards they receive. One can also act to increase one's own outcomes—an action that can sometimes take the form of dishonest behavior. For example, Greenberg (1993) conducted an experiment in which college students were given the opportunity to steal from an experimenter. He found that students were more likely to steal from an experimenter who paid them less than they had been promised than from an experimenter who made the promised payment.

College students' stated reasons for academic dishonesty often reflect the view that dishonesty is a legitimate response to what they perceive to be unfair treatment by an instructor, and students report cheating more often in classes conducted by instructors whom they believe treat them unfairly (Whitley, 1998). Consequently, instructors may be able to reduce students' motivation to cheat by ensuring that an atmosphere of fairness prevails in their classrooms. Rodabaugh (1996), who has extensively studied the causes and effects of students' perceptions of fairness in the classroom, has identified three major aspects of fairness that are of concern to students: *Interactional fairness* concerns the nature of the interaction between instructor and student, *procedural fairness* concerns the establishment and enforcement of rules for grading and classroom administration, and *outcome fairness* concerns the distribution of grades. Box 3.1 provides examples of each of these types of fairness.

Interactional Fairness

You might expect that students would be most concerned with outcome or procedural fairness because it affects their grades. However, Rodabaugh (1996) found that students consider violations of interactional fairness to be the most severe. There are five aspects to interactional fairness: impartiality, respect, concern for students, integrity, and propriety.

Impartiality. Students expect their instructors to treat everyone in the class equally. Although it is unlikely that many instructors intentionally favor some students over others, it is probably impossible not to like some students more than others. Differences in liking are apt to lead to differences in interacting with students, such as calling on some students to answer questions more frequently than others or allowing some students to dominate discussions. Such differences in the way in which students are

BOX 3.1
Inequities Illustrated

Based on student interviews, we offer three accounts that illustrate interactional, procedural, and outcome fairness, respectively. In all three cases, the students reported that cheating was so rampant that they succumbed just to pass the course.

- A high school English teacher often yelled at the entire class. Her favorite line was, "What language are you people speaking?" She presented material at such a fast pace that most students did not understand it, but she was brusque with any student who asked a question or requested a clarification. Disgusted students actively assisted each other with homework assignments and papers that were supposed to be completed independently and worked out a passing system to help each other during exams.
- Students in a college history course resented the instructor's heavy reliance on 10 quizzes with no opportunity to make up any that were missed. The quizzes were worth 50% of the grade. In the syllabus handed out on the first day of class, however, the quizzes were listed as being worth only 20% of the grade with no mention of a no-makeup policy. The instructor explained, "I changed my mind about the weight that the quizzes carry, and my new policy will help assure that you attend class regularly."
- The professor told his algebra class on the first day of school that he gives only two or three As each semester, and most students will get Cs, Ds, and Fs. He also has a reputation for picking favorite students to whom he directs most of his attention, and the other students suspect that his grading criteria involves other than math ability.

treated may lead to perceptions of partiality even when no such partiality exists. For example, Keith-Spiegel et al. (1993) found that 90% of the students they surveyed thought that an instructor "being more friendly to some students than to others" was inappropriate in at least a minor degree, and 45% thought that it would be inappropriate under many or all circumstances. Therefore, instructors should carefully monitor their behavior to avoid giving the impression of partiality.

Respect. Respect involves treating students politely. Keith-Spiegel et al. (1993) found that 85% of their student respondents thought that an instructor ridiculing a student or referring to a student's comment as "stupid" was inappropriate in many or all circumstances. Similarly, Rodabaugh (1996) found that students expect a instructor to listen to, carefully consider, and give thoughtful replies to their ideas when they challenge the instructor's views on a topic. As frustrating as the comments, questions, and work quality of some students may be, patience is the best response. If students perceive an instructor to be demeaning to them or other students either directly through comments or indirectly through tone of voice, facial expressions, or posture, they lose respect for the instructor. In addition, they may see dishonesty as a way of getting even by showing disrespect for something the instructor values. Academic integrity may be the target of choice.

It may be especially difficult to be patient with students who actively misbehave in class, such as by talking to friends, reading newspapers, and so forth. However, Keith-Spiegel et al. (1993) found that students expect instructors to also deal with those kinds of situations in a polite manner. For example, 45% of students thought that it was inappropriate for an instructor to "humiliate a student for falling asleep in class" in many or all circumstances. Instructors should therefore try to remain civil and calm even in the face of apparent disrespect, thereby modeling the appropriate behavior for students. It is always appropriate to call an offending student in for a private confrontation during which one can be more direct in communicating expectations for student deportment in the classroom.

Concern for Students. As shown in chapter 2, one reason students give for engaging in academic dishonesty is that instructors do not care about them or their academic performance. Conversely, Stern and Havlicek (1986) found students thought that an increase in individual interactions between instructors and students would probably reduce academic misconduct. One can demonstrate concern for students by learning and using their names, talking to them before and after class, carefully answering questions, and inviting students who appear to be having problems with the course to discuss those problems and potential solutions. Concern is also reflected in giving due consideration to student complaints, taking remedial action when the complaints are valid, and carefully explaining one's position when the complaints are not valid (Rodabaugh, 1996).

Showing concern for students is especially difficult when teaching large classes, which can enroll 500 or more students in some universities. Nonetheless, there are measures you can take to make students feel welcome and cared for. Some suggestions are shown in Box 3.2. Another situation in which it can be difficult to make psychological contact with students is during televised distance education classes. Box 3.3 provides some suggestions for establishing rapport with distance education students.

BOX 3.2
Establishing Personal Contact With Students in Large Classes

- Tell the class a little about your personal and professional background.
- Use a remote microphone and audiovisual controls so that you can walk around the room. Ask students questions and give them the mike to respond.
- On the first day of class, have students introduce themselves to the people sitting next to them.
- Have students periodically fill out feedback sheets that allow them to express opinions and ask questions about the course. Respond to these during the next class meeting.
- When you attend professional meetings, especially if you have to miss class, tell the students a little about what happened at the meeting.
- Arrive early for class and stay a little time after class so that you can talk to students in the hall or in the classroom.
- Give students your e-mail address and encourage comments and questions. Reply promptly to the student and discuss selected messages with the class (keeping the sender anonymous, of course).
- Use as many collaborative and small-group exercises and discussions as are feasible.
- Be proactive about inviting students to visit during office hours.
- Schedule help sessions in which you, not just tutors or teaching assistants, participate.

From "Can the Academic Integrity of Cost-Effective Distance Learning Course Offerings Be Protected?" by Mary Elisabeth Randall in Dana D. Burnett, Lynn Rudolph, & Karen O. Clifford (Eds.), *Academic Integrity Matters.* Copyright 1998 by the National Association of Student Personnel Administrators. Adapted with permission.

Integrity. Integrity means being consistent and truthful in explaining one's policies, procedures, and decisions so that their fairness can be judged. Truthfulness includes such practices as explaining policies and procedures completely and clearly, delivering promised rewards and penalties, and admitting ignorance when appropriate. Explanation simply means telling students why policies and procedures exist, especially when the policies or procedures may appear to students to be unfair. For example, one could explain an attendance policy by pointing out that attendance is correlated with increased learning and better grades. One could also explain the educational goals of various types of assignments, and such

BOX 3.3
Establishing Personal Contact With Distance Education Students

- Request that students send photographs of themselves to you; when a student is participating over the audio link, display that student's photograph on the classroom camera so that students at other sites can see what the student looks like.
- Code students' names by location and call on students at each location at least once per class session.
- Try to visit each site at which the course is offered at least once during the term to meet informally with students.
- Offer open microphones before classes begin or just after they end to encourage questions and conversations.
- Provide call-in office hours exclusively for distance education students.

Note. Adapted from Randall (1998, p. 128).

explanations can be effective. Greenberg (1990) found that complete explanation of what people initially perceive as unfair policies and practices can lead to acceptance of them.

Propriety. Propriety means acting in a socially acceptable manner, obeying the rules of proper behavior, and avoiding offending students' sensibilities. Students expect their instructor to follow the rules when interacting with them even if the instructor believes there might be pedagogical value in breaking the rules. Thus, Keith-Spiegel et al. (1993) found that 53% of their student respondents thought that it was inappropriate for an instructor to tell an off-color story or joke in most or all circumstances, and 80% thought the same about showing an emotionally upsetting film without warning students about it in advance. Students also expect instructors to respect their privacy: 88% thought that it was inappropriate to require students to reveal highly personal information in a class discussion. Finally, students expect instructors to maintain an appropriate social distance: 54% thought that it was inappropriate for an instructor to date a student, and 70% thought that it was inappropriate for an instructor to have a sexual relationship with a student.

Procedural Fairness

Students rate procedural fairness second in importance to interaction fairness and higher than outcome (grading) fairness (Rodabaugh, 1996). As Rodabaugh noted, "students, like the general population, assume that if the procedures for determining outcomes are fair, then the outcomes will be fair" (p. 39). Four factors contribute to perceived procedural fairness in the classroom: course work load, tests, feedback, and provision for student input.

Course Work Load. As noted in chapter 2, one reason students give for engaging in academic dishonesty is an inability to keep up with the work in the course. Research has found that students who report heavier work loads are more likely to report engaging in academic dishonesty (Whitley, 1998). Although many factors (e.g., employment, involvement in extracurricular activities, low aptitude for the type of work done in the course) can lead students to perceive a work load as too heavy when it is in fact reasonable, course work loads can sometimes actually be too heavy. This problem may be especially likely to arise in fields where the knowledge base is rapidly expanding and teachers feel pressured to include more and more material in the same 45 or so classroom hours in a term. If instructors feel pressed to cover everything they want to cover in a course, the students may feel overloaded as well. When such pressure exists, it might be time to review the course content with an eye to pruning it back.

It is important to take student ability into account when designing a course. A course designed for the general student population should be less technical than one designed for students majoring in the field. When teaching first-year students, it is also important to bear in mind that most will be learning study skills along with the content of the course, and the difficulty of the course and of its tests and assignments should be calibrated accordingly (e.g., Erickson & Strommer, 1991).

Tests. As we saw in the last chapter, students say that unfair tests motivate cheating. What makes a test appear fair to students? Three factors contribute to this perception. One is that all the material on the test is relevant to the course and was covered in lectures, readings, or both. If one reuses test questions, it is easy to forget to double-check them to ensure their currency when revising lectures or changing textbooks. A second factor is that the test is at an appropriate level of difficulty for the course. As with work load, the proper level of test difficulty can vary as a function of the student population to which the course is directed. Students are especially offended when tests seem to be intentionally designed to flunk people out of the course, thus reducing the size of the class or the number of majors in a department for faculty convenience (e.g., Keith-Spiegel et al., 1993). Consequently, students may feel especially justified in cheating on such tests. A final factor is that the test is well designed with clearly phrased questions; on multiple-choice tests, response options should be clearly phrased. Gronlund (1993) and Ory and Ryan (1993) provided excellent advice on the construction of classroom tests.

Providing Feedback. As well as being a pedagogically sound practice, providing prompt and constructive feedback on the results of tests and assignments leads students to perceive instructors as fair and concerned about their progress (Rodabaugh, 1996). Feedback should include not only telling students what questions they got right and what questions they got wrong, but also explaining why the wrong answers are incorrect, especially for items that are missed by a substantial proportion of students. As Rodabaugh noted, this process takes up relatively little time even in large classes while providing large dividends in terms of student good will.

Being Responsive to Students. Not only should instructors provide feedback *to* students, but they should also solicit and be responsive to feedback *from* students. For example, instructors should give serious consideration to student complaints that a test question was ambiguous or might have more than one correct answer, and they should take remedial action when such complaints are valid. Instructors should also ensure that students understand assignments, soliciting and answering questions about requirements, procedures, deadlines, and so forth when distributing the assignment. In general, students should feel they have a reasonable level of control over their outcomes in the class rather than feel they are mere pawns being manipulated by the instructor (Whitley & Kite, 1998).

Outcome Fairness

Like it or not, grades are an important part of higher education and an important component of student perceptions of fairness and thus of their academic integrity. Students want their grades to accurately reflect their performance; if students feel unfairly deprived of the grades they think they deserve, many will cheat to obtain what they see as their just due. The following list provides some guidelines on how to grade fairly; it is drawn from the perspectives of both faculty (Ory & Ryan, 1993) and students (Rodabaugh, 1996).

1. *Follow institutional practice.* A department, college, or university may have specific policies concerning the proportion of As, Bs, Cs, and so on that may be given in a class. If no formal policy exists, the actual distributions of grades in similar courses provide informal guidelines. Students compare their grades with those of their peers and are likely to feel cheated if their grades are low compared with other students in similar courses being taught by other instructors. A student who feels cheated may reciprocate by cheating.

2. *Use accurate assessment instruments.* Assessment instruments—tests, term papers, homework, presentations, and other assignments—should yield accurate information about student performance. Therefore, one should continually review and update assessment instruments to ensure their accuracy. For example, the questions in test banks supplied by textbook publishers are often written by someone other than the textbook authors. As a result, those questions are sometimes poorly constructed because the question writer (often a graduate student) does not fully understand the textbook material, is on a short deadline, or for other reasons. One of us even once found a question on information that was not included in the textbook. Therefore, you should always check test bank questions against the book. Similarly, if you reuse test questions, you should check them when changing textbooks or when moving to a new edition of a textbook you currently use.

Poorly worded exam and quiz questions, such as those that are ambiguous or include terms not covered in class or in assigned readings, also reduce the accuracy of assessment. It can be useful to have a student who has already completed the course read your questions for clarity.

3. *Make multiple assessments.* Students are better at some academic tasks than others: Some students do better on objective tests, whereas others do better on term papers or essay tests. Consequently, accurate evaluation of student performance provides students with a variety of ways to show their learning so that strengths can offset weaknesses. Similarly, multiple tests, essays, and so forth provide more accurate information about student

performance than just one measure. A student having a bad day when the only exam in a course is given does not have a fair chance to demonstrate her or his abilities.

4. *Tell students how they will be graded.* The course syllabus should inform students about what assessment instruments will be used and how much weight each will have in determining the course grade. Students should also be told how grades will be determined, such as being based on preset cutoff scores that are listed for them or based on their relative ranking in the class (grading "on the curve").

5. *Grade based on individual performance.* Students want their grades to reflect their performance, not other people's. In this regard, grades based on preset cutoffs may be more satisfying to students than grades based on relative performance, but the use of preset cutoffs may be disadvantageous for other reasons. For example, students may be more likely to report classmates they see cheating if the course is graded "on the curve" because their grade could be negatively affected by cheaters. Students may feel less compunction about cheating, however, when grades are assigned on an absolute basis because their behavior will not affect their classmates' grades. Students also prefer to be graded individually for their contribution to group work. Consequently, it is useful to include such assessments into a grading scheme, such as by using peer assessments or requiring individual papers based on collaborative assignments.

6. *Don't change policies midcourse.* Students expect grading policies to be firm, so changes should be avoided except in the most unusual circumstances. However, if alterations must be made, the changes and reasons for them should be fully explained. In addition, the new policies should ideally be beneficial to students, such as adding an opportunity to gain points toward final grades. At the very least, alterations in policies should at least balance costs and benefits.

One of the best means of ensuring that students perceive an instructor to be fair, especially in terms of procedures and outcomes, is a complete syllabus. A syllabus should contain not only an outline of the course, but also a complete description of all the course's ground rules. For example, in the context of grading, what number of points or percentage of the final grade will come from each test, paper, homework assignment, and so forth? If contributions to class discussions are graded, exactly what does *contribution* mean and how will its quality be assessed? If extra credit is allowed, how much is it worth and how do students earn it? Due dates and any penalties for late assignments should be clearly described. The syllabus should also contain information on procedural issues, such as the degree to which students are allowed to collaborate on assignments and the kinds of assistance they are allowed to have. To reemphasize a point we made before, remember: Unless students are specifically told what they can and cannot do, they will assume that anything not explicitly forbidden is permitted.

The syllabus is a contract between the instructor and the students enrolled in a course. Like any contract, the more complete and explicit the syllabus is, the less room exists for varying interpretations. Consequently, there is less likelihood that students will perceive the instructor to be interpreting an individual situation in an unfair manner. Do not assume that students understand what constitutes academic dishonesty. The syllabus may also be a critical exhibit in an academic dishonesty hearing (see the first case in Box 3.4).

We recommend that each class syllabus contain the following eight elements. Some sample statements for each of the elements may be found in Appendix 3.1.

1. A brief, general statement about the importance of academic integrity in higher education.
2. A personal statement declaring your commitment to upholding academic honesty in your classes.
3. How you will deal with any incidents that you observe or that come to your attention.
4. A brief list of the types of academic dishonesty in your school's policy (or reference to where the complete policy can be found).
5. A brief list of any types of academic dishonesty that could occur in your particular course that could benefit from more detail (e.g., oral plagiarism in a class that requires an oral report).
6. A brief list of campus resources that may help reduce the risk factors associated with cheating (e.g., writing clinic, counseling center, learning center or tutoring program).
7. An invitation to come directly to you to discuss anything that it unclear or confusing regarding the appropriate way to complete assignments.
8. An invitation to report incidents of academic dishonesty.

BOX 3.4
When Pointing Out the Obvious Is Still Worth Doing

BEING OBVIOUS ABOUT COLLABORATION

A colleague of ours was confident that the discovery of two identical research reports constituted an obvious case of academic dishonesty—either unpermitted collaboration or plagiarism from one student by the other. When she called the two students into her office to discuss the matter, they blamed our friend for not making her policies clear. The students also rejected our colleague's decision to assign each a grade of F on the assignment and opted instead for a formal hearing. Again, the students claimed that our colleague had not clearly specified that copying from each other was forbidden. Although the hearing panel found in our colleague's favor, one member later confided to her that it was her syllabus—which clearly specified that assignments must be each student's independent work—that was a primary factor in the panel's decision.

BEING OBVIOUS ABOUT HOW TO ANSWER TEST QUESTIONS

Another colleague told us about a problem that arose on a multiple-choice test. Ten students had gotten together earlier and decided it might be advantageous to fill in two or three choices for questions they weren't sure about. Because our colleague had never explicitly stated in her syllabus, in class, or in the test instructions that students could not choose more than one answer, she felt she could not punish them as severely as they deserved. She gave each student a failing grade on the test. She also told the class about the incident (without naming the students involved), expressed her disappointment with the class over the incident, and invited any students who wanted to discuss the incident to see her in her office. Many of the students who came to talk to her about it were annoyed about the leniency of the punishment. Our colleague's syllabi now includes a statement regarding the appropriate way to answer multiple-choice questions.

DISCUSSING ACADEMIC INTEGRITY

In addition to working to ensure fairness in the classroom, instructors can foster academic integrity by discussing it with their students. By *discussion* we mean a complete explanation by the instructor plus input and feedback from students. Simply saying "Don't cheat" may or may not have an effect on students' behavior (e.g., Aiken, 1991; Kerkvliet & Sigmund, 1999). However, classroom discussions of academic integrity appear to be uncommon. Nuss (1984) found that only about half the faculty members she surveyed reported making even a cursory mention of academic integrity issues in their classes. Perhaps instructors assume that students are getting the message from other sources. Kibler (1994) found that almost all the colleges and universities he surveyed included information about academic integrity in their student handbooks, but that only 69% included it as part of new student orientation programs and only 62% included it in their catalogs. More proactive efforts are rarer. Kibler found that only 36% of the institutions he surveyed offered seminars or discussions of academic integrity issues, and only 22% required that information on these topics be included in course syllabi. Consequently, students are least likely to hear about academic integrity issues where they are most likely to pay attention—in the classroom.

Similarly, books for students on the topic of how to succeed in college rarely provide students with guidance on academic integrity issues. We have seen only one (Jewler, Gardner, & McCarthy, 1993) that does so.

Perhaps instructors and handbook authors assume that students just do not want to hear about academic integrity or they just do not care. After all, aren't today's college students supposed to be part of the alienated and apathetic Generation X? Maybe not. Consider the experience of Yale Law School Professor Stephen Carter:

> A couple of years ago I began a university commencement address by telling the audience that I was going to talk about integrity. The crowd broke into applause. Applause! Just because they had heard the word integrity—that's how starved for it they were. They had no idea how I was using the word, or what I was going to say about it, or, indeed, whether I was for it or against it. But they knew they liked the idea of simply talking about it. (Carter, 1996, pp. 5–6)

Discussion Goals

Drawing on theories of organizational communication, Roth and McCabe (1995) suggested that one factor leading to academic dishonesty is a lack of agreement between instructors and students on what behaviors constitute academic dishonesty and how severe a violation of integrity those behaviors are. We saw in the last chapter that there are, in fact, a number of behaviors that faculty consider to be dishonest but that students do not, and that faculty and students do not always agree on the severity of a particular behavior. In addition, Roth and McCabe found that students who agreed with their university's definition of cheating and with the appropriateness of the university's punishments for cheating were less likely to cheat on exams than were other students. The goal of discussions of academic integrity, then, is to try to align student and faculty perceptions of what academic integrity and academic dishonesty are and how dishonesty should be handled.

We realize that perfect alignment of student and faculty views on academic integrity may be an unattainable ideal under many circumstances. For example, such alignment may be easier in colleges and universities with honor codes and with campus cultures in which academic integrity plays a central role (e.g., McCabe & Trevino, 1993). Nevertheless, we believe that such discussions can be useful under most circumstances for two reasons. First, alignment of views cannot occur without discussion; although discussion may not be sufficient for alignment of views, it is certainly necessary. Second, even when people disagree with the policies and procedures promulgated by those in positions of authority, such as instructors, they are more likely to accept and comply with those policies and procedures when they understand their purpose (e.g., Greenberg, 1990). Consequently, even if some students' views of academic dishonesty do not agree with the instructor's views by the end of the discussion, those students may still comply with the instructor's requirements.

Discussion Content

What should one cover when discussing academic integrity with students? We suggest three topics: the importance of integrity, institutional policies on academic integrity and dishonesty, and the instructor's personal policies.

The Importance of Integrity. In chapter 1, we discussed some of the reasons that academic integrity is important. These reasons can be used to organize a class discussion of academic integrity. Students also often provide reasons of their own. It might also interest students to know that academic dishonesty is correlated with other forms of dishonesty, including petty theft, lying to boyfriends and girlfriends, and dealing dishonestly with bosses, coworkers, subordinates, and customers on the job (Blankenship & Whitley, 2000). In short, people who cheat in college tend to cheat in other aspects of their lives as well. In our experience in presenting integrity information to students, this fact appears to impress them profoundly, generating considerable discussion. Carter (1996) provides an excellent introduction to the general concept of integrity and discusses a number of nonacademic examples.

Institutional Policies. Although students may, in theory, know their institution's policies on academic integrity from such sources as catalogs and student handbooks (Kibler, 1994), you should not assume such knowledge. Students may not have read the policies or may not remember them. Even those students who have read the policies may not understand them. Data collected on two campuses reveal that only 1 student in 20 believed he or she had a working knowledge of their school's academic honesty policy (Keith-Spiegel & Gray-Shellberg, 1997). Therefore, one should inform students, preferably in writing, of:

1. What behaviors constitute academic dishonesty.
2. The responsibilities students have (if any) to prevent or report others' academic dishonesty.
3. The administrative procedures that will be followed if a student is suspected of academic dishonesty.

The Instructor's Own Policies. Finally, instructors should inform students of their personal policies. As discussed in more detail in the next chapter, these policies *must* be consistent with institutional policies. However, personal policies vary somewhat from instructor to instructor when institutional policies allow latitude. It is especially important to inform students if collaboration is allowed on assignments and, if so, what forms it may take: Students are likely to assume that collaboration is allowed unless it is specifically forbidden. Box 3.5 presents a sticky situation faced by two of our own students. Finally, let students know what penalties will be assessed by you in cases of academic dishonesty; we discuss the issue of penalties in more detail in chapter 5.

FACILITATING STUDENT LEARNING

As noted in chapter 2, the reasons students give for engaging in academic dishonesty indicate that the temptation is greater when they view a course or assignment as meaningless or unfair or when they lack the confidence that they can succeed without cheating. In addition, research also indicates that students who believe they will fail otherwise are more likely to engage in academic dishonesty (Whitley, 1998). Consequently, the more you can do to ensure that students know and understand the material covered in

BOX 3.5
The Importance of Being Clear

Two of our students who, ironically, had been enthusiastic contributors in an academic integrity seminar came to us in tears. They had just been told that they were about to be formally charged with cheating in the form of unauthorized collaboration on a take-home final examination. The students did not dispute that they had, indeed, heavily conferred with each other and shared resources during the process of writing out their exams. They claimed, however, that the instructor had told them that they were allowed to help each other and to consult any resource. The instructor's response was, "Well, yes, you could help each other but when it came time to actually write out the exam, you had to be alone and on your own. That should have been obvious."

Unfortunately for everyone concerned, the conditions under which the final exam was to be taken did not appear in the syllabus. This case was eventually resolved informally. The students were able to persuade the instructor that the rules were unclear and offered to do whatever the instructor required to redo the assignment. The instructor offered them the option of taking another essay exam, separately, in his office. The students accepted this solution. The instructor revised the section of his syllabus to precisely describe the rules for taking the final exams.

---

the course, the less the students' temptation to cheat will be. In this section we offer a few general suggestions for improving student learning divided into two parts: what can be done in class and what can be done outside of class. College teaching handbooks, both general ones and those designed for particular disciplines, offer a wealth of suggestions and are well worth perusing.

In Class

Explain the Relevance of What Students Do. Students who do not understand the purpose of a course or assignment are more likely to cheat than are those who do. Therefore, it is important to ensure that students understand how a course, especially one that is difficult and required, fits into the curriculum as a whole and how the skills learned in the course can be applied to real life. Similarly, students need to know how particular assignments contribute to the learning objectives of the course. Although these reasons are obvious to instructors, students often have not yet acquired the knowledge or experience to make the necessary connections on their own.

We are also concerned that many students do not appreciate the value of knowledge. Box 3.6 provides an example of the kind of story that might help contemporary students more fully appreciate the merit of a well-rounded education in addition to proficiency in one's major.

Teach Necessary Skills. Instructors must ensure that students have the skills needed to succeed in the course. Sometimes one can assume that skills will be taught in prerequisite courses. However, unless the skills are an explicit part of the prerequisite, one should not assume that students have acquired them. Even if the skills are taught in a prerequisite course, students may need a review to refresh their memories.

An important case in point is plagiarism. As noted in chapter 2, Roig (1997) found that students often cannot differentiate between plagiarized and paraphrased text. In addition, he found that students generally do not know how to paraphrase material, and that more difficult material is less likely to be paraphrased properly (Roig, 1999). Although one might expect students to be taught how to paraphrase as part of their writing courses, Drum (1987) noted that writing textbooks generally do not discuss paraphrasing and that many college composition classes fail to cover the topic adequately. In addition, students may not know how to do the research necessary to write a paper without plagiarizing it. McLeod (1992) noted, for example, that "Students often come to us from high schools where they have written papers by carefully copying information from encyclopedias. . . . But that strategy no longer works for them in college, and students must not only have to learn new strategies, they have to un-learn the old" (p. 12). Consequently, instructors who assign papers that require the use of source material must teach their students how to avoid plagiarism. Box 3.7 contains some suggestions for helping students avoid plagiarism (Wilhoit, 1994). Appendix 3.2 offers additional information that may help implement some of the suggestions offered in Box 3.7, and Box 3.8 lists some web sites that provide guidelines to students on avoiding plagiarism.

Teach at the Appropriate Level. As noted earlier, the type of course material that is appropriate for some students, such as advanced students and those majoring in a field, may be too difficult for others, such as first-year students and those not majoring in the field. Because students who

BOX 3.6
The Career That Was Won With the Civil War

A student of mine told me this story years after he took my course on the Civil War. He was a business major and recalled resenting having to learn "old stuff about dead people." After he earned his degree, he went out for job interviews. The job market was tight, but he was excited to get an invitation to interview with the manager of a firm in the city where he wanted to live. He saw a Civil War battle print on the manager's wall and made a comment about it. A conversation about the Civil War ensued. The manager, it turns out, was a Civil War buff. The student was offered the job and believes that it was his passing knowledge about the Civil War that made him stand out from the others.

Note. (Miguel Dominguez, interview with Patricia Keith-Spiegel, May 1997.)

believe the course material is too difficult may be tempted to academic dishonesty, it is important to match the difficulty of the course material and textbook to the abilities of the students for whom the course is intended.

We recognize that today's students are a very heterogeneous group, and deciding exactly what level to target can be tricky. In small classes, extra opportunities might be offered to enrich the course experience for the more able or motivated students, allowing the less-able students to more easily keep up with the regular course requirements. The syllabus and first class day should provide enough information about the course requirements to allow students who may not be well suited to select themselves out.

Provide Study Guides. As knowledge expands and textbooks become more encyclopedic, the traditional student question of "What's really important?" becomes more relevant. Students, sometimes realistically, believe they cannot learn everything in the textbook, and instructors often believe that some aspects of the material are more important or relevant than others. Thus, one way to give students a sense of confidence that they are studying the relevant material and to help them study more efficiently is provide study guides that point them in the right direction. Although there is no research on the effectiveness of study guides in preventing academic dishonesty, Hollinger and Lanza-Kaduce (1996) found that 55% of the students they surveyed thought that study guides would help prevent

BOX 3.7
Helping Students Avoid Plagiarism

- Define and discuss plagiarism thoroughly.
- Discuss hypothetical cases of writers encountering problems as they compose papers. For example, if a friend reads over a draft of a paper and suggests changes, is it plagiarism to include those changes without citing them as the friend's ideas?
- Give students a source text to read along with summaries of the text, some of which represent plagiarism and some of which represent proper paraphrasing. Have students identify the plagiarized passages, explain why they represent plagiarism, and correct them so they are correctly paraphrased.
- Teach proper note-taking skills, such as how to properly annotate quotations on note cards.
- Teach students how to correctly quote and document sources. Because the rules of documentation can differ somewhat from discipline to discipline, clearly explain what should be done in *your* class.
- Pace students through the paper-writing process by requiring them to turn in intermediate products, such as topic ideas, partial bibliographies, the introductory section of the paper, and so forth, at appropriate points during the term. This policy will act as a spur to students who might procrastinate and then resort to plagiarism as a means to catch up.
- Require students to turn in rough drafts and revisions of their papers along with the final version. This requirement will discourage students from turning in papers that they borrowed or purchased. (Students could, of course, fake the drafts, but many students would probably see that as being more trouble than it's worth.)
- Require students to submit photocopies of cited sources. This requirement will cause students to take more care in properly citing sources and discourage outright plagiarism because access to the source material is needed.
- Provide students with guidelines to follow for identifying unintentional plagiarism when proofreading their papers (e.g., missing quotation marks, missing or inaccurate documentation). A checklist can be especially helpful.
- Provide students with guidelines for collaboration when collaboration is allowed or required.
- If you detect what appears to be plagiarism, work with the student to correct his or her mistakes. Approach the situation as a teaching opportunity rather than as an occasion for punishment.

Note. From *College Teaching*, vol. 42 no. 4, pp. 162–163, 1994. Reprinted with permission of the Helen Dwight Reid Educational Foundation. Published by Heldref Publications, 1319 18th St. N.W. Washington, DC 20036–1802. Copyright 1994.

BOX 3.8
Some Web Sites to Help Students Avoid Plagiarism

Hamilton College
> http://www.hamilton.edu/academic/Resource/WC/AvoidingPlagiarism.html

Indiana University
> http://www.indiana.edu/~wts/wts/plagiarism.html

Northwestern University
> http://www.northwestern.edu/uacc/plagiar.html

University of California, Davis
> http://sja.ucdavis.edu/SJA/plagiarism.html

University of Wisconsin–Milwaukee
> http://www.uwm.edu/People//pcsmith/author1.htm

Vanguard University of Southern California
> http://www.vanguard.edu/rharris/antiplag.htm

Note. URLs were valid as of March 16, 2001.

cheating. They also found this opinion to be more prevalent among students who had cheated than those who had not.

Invite Questions. Because students may not completely grasp material the first time it is presented, it is important to provide them with ample opportunity to ask questions about the material covered in lectures and the textbook. As we have noted, students who feel confident about their understanding of course material are less prone to academic dishonesty. In addition, because behavior that appears to constitute academic dishonesty can result from misunderstandings, one should also provide opportunities for questions concerning the requirements for assignments, the nature of tests, and so forth. In addition, students may be reluctant to ask questions because they are afraid of looking stupid, so one should periodically invite them to ask questions. For these invitations to be effective, they should be carefully phrased. A key point is to avoid implying that students should not have questions, such as by saying, "You don't have any questions, do you?" Rather, the invitation should imply that questions are expected, such as by saying, "What questions do you have?"

Another strategy to elicit questions is to periodically distribute 3 x 5-inch cards to class. Ask the students to write down any questions they have and then collect the cards and answer the questions. Students who are reluctant to ask a question in public might feel comfortable asking it anonymously.

Outside of Class

Hold Tutoring Sessions. Periodic tutoring or question-answering sessions outside of class can help students gain the confidence that they can perform well without cheating. Although such sessions can be effectively run by teaching assistants or student volunteers, if the instructor attends at least some sessions it enhances students' perceptions that the instructor cares about their progress in the course (Rodabaugh, 1996). Such perceptions may also deter cheating.

Be Available to Students. Establishing generous office hours (and show-ing up for them) also provides the instructor with opportunities to both help students and show concern for them. If one has teaching assistants, it is also important to ensure their availability to students outside of class. If an office hour must be missed, announce it in advance if at all possible. Along with providing helpful information, such announcements remind students that you respect them and their schedules. Attempt to offer alternatives to those students who have classes during your office hours. Now that most students and faculty use electronic mail, connections can be made in this way: Ask students to e-mail the times they are available so you can set up an appointment that is convenient for them. Our experience has been that students are very impressed with instructors who promptly respond to their e-mail inquires.

Identify and Refer Students at Risk for Dishonesty. Another way to foster academic integrity is to identify students who may be at higher than average risk for dishonesty and assist them in avoiding dishonesty. In his literature review, Whitley (1998) identified several characteristics that could be used to identify students at risk for dishonesty. These characteristics include:

- poor study skills,
- low levels of industriousness and high levels of procrastination,
- high test anxiety,

- poor class attendance, and
- a high degree of involvement in extracurricular activities.

These factors are likely to result in marginal academic performance, which has a fairly high association with cheating. For example, Houston (1978; Houston & Ziff, 1976) found that students who are on the border between passing and failing are most likely to cheat and are most likely to see cheating as an effective means of getting a higher score. Instructors can monitor students for these risk indicators and facilitate both learning and academic skills development for these students by referring them to specialized resources such as college or university learning centers, writing tutors, and study skills programs.

REDUCING PRESSURE ON STUDENTS

Students report that pressure for high grades—either from parents or a perceived need for high grades to get a job or gain admission to graduate or professional school—is one factor that motivates academic dishonesty. In this section, we briefly discuss four steps instructors might consider as ways to reduce achievement pressure on students: use multiple sources of evaluation, provide information about tests, allow students to be retested and to redo assignments, and reduce competition for grades.

Use Multiple Means of Evaluation

As we noted earlier, some students are better at some academic tasks, such as tests, whereas other students are better at others, such as term papers or essays. Using a variety of means of evaluating students' progress makes it more likely that students will encounter forms of evaluation that are more comfortable for them. This comfort level will help reduce performance anxiety and the accompanying motivation for academic dishonesty. It is also useful, especially in introductory courses, to use several tests, papers, and other assignments in a course rather than just one or two. The less weight any one evaluation situation contributes to the final grade, the more likely students are to feel that they can make up a poor performance on a future evaluation or that they are not losing everything if they do poorly on one assignment. In addition to reducing performance pressures and students' motivation to cheat, the use of multiple means of evaluation provides a more accurate assessment of their knowledge and skills (e.g., Ory & Ryan, 1993).

Provide Information About Tests

Tests are the form of evaluation that perhaps elicit the greatest performance anxiety in students: Not only must they perform well, but they must do so under time pressure. Consequently, students have devised a large number of creative ways to cheat on tests (Cizek, 1999). In addition to the difficulties inherent in test taking, students must cope with each instructor's own testing style. Testing styles reflect preferences in question type (such as essay vs. multiple choice), types of questions (such as definitions vs. theory vs. application), and which aspects of the material covered by the test are essential for students to know and are therefore testable. Testing style can influence students' performance. Once they learn an instructor's style, such as by taking the first test in a course, they feel more comfortable about taking the instructor's tests, can better prepare for future tests, and can perform better on future tests (e.g., Whitley, 1996). Consequently, the more students know about what is and is not testable and the nature of the test questions, the more confident they will be about the test and the less motivation they may have to cheat.

There are several things instructors can do to inform students about their testing styles. One technique already discussed is the provision of study guides for both textbook and lecture material. Another technique is giving students sample questions that accurately reflect the instructor's testing style. Perhaps a more effective technique is allowing students to review old test questions when exams are changed: Even when the questions are different, the instructor's testing style is consistent. For example, Hollinger and Lanza-Kaduce (1996), found that 52% of the students they surveyed thought that passing out old exams would be an effective deterrent to cheating; as with the utility of study guides, this opinion was more prevalent among students who had cheated than among those who had not.

Erickson and Strommer (1991) went a step further and suggested distributing the stems of multiple-choice questions that will actually appear on the exam. Although this procedure may appear to make the test meaningless, Erickson and Strommer pointed out that tests of understanding and thinking are not compromised by distributing question stems such as:

Which of the following statements best characterizes Freud's view of the relation between society and the individual?

It is often said that humans are social animals. Suppose someone said this to Freud. Which of the following statements best represents his most likely response? (p. 158).

Question stems such as these do not provide direct cues to the answers. As part of the study process, students must think about the material and prepare their own answers as they would as part of an essay exam. Consequently, they may learn the material better, with better learning being reflected as enhanced test performance and less motivation to cheat.

Allow Students to Be Retested and to Redo Assignments

Allowing students the opportunity to be retested on material (using new questions) and redo assignments reduces performance anxiety because students know that if they perform poorly because of illness or other handicapping factors they will have the opportunity to show what they really know. One drawback of using this technique for exams is that multiple forms of each test are required. Another negative feature is that it may engender procrastination. That is, students may do poorly the first time because they failed to study adequately knowing that they had another chance. However, allowing students to be retested and redo assignments may be worth the effort not only in terms of reducing students' motivations for cheating, but also because it enhances learning (e.g., Bloom, 1984; Fitzgerald, 1987).

Reduce Competition for Grades

Whitley (1998) found that greater competition for grades in a class was associated with higher levels of cheating: If high grades are a valued but a rare commodity, students will cheat to get them. The temptation to cheat may be especially great if the number of high grades is artificially limited by the use of norm-referenced grading or grading "on the curve." Because the number of students who receive each grade is limited, high-ability students may receive lower grades than they deserve and average ability students may receive failing grades. Students anticipating grades lower than they deserve may cheat to get the higher grade, thereby, of course, pushing other students down the grade ladder.

One solution to this problem is the use of absolute grading standards: A cutoff score is established in advance for each grade and any student who meets the cutoff score receives the grade. Absolute grading systems can be difficult to construct and require careful attention to the design of tests and other evaluation instruments (Ory & Ryan, 1993). However, such systems do have advantages in addition to potentially lowering the motivation for cheating: They require the instructor to clearly define course goals and standards, they result in grades that reflect actual achievement levels, and they promote a cooperative classroom climate in which students help each other learn (Ory & Ryan, 1993).

COURSE-SPECIFIC HONOR SYSTEMS

As noted in chapters 1 and 2, research has indicated that college and universities with honor codes have lower cheating rates than do similar colleges and universities without honor codes. Does this mean that establishing an honor system for your own courses will reduce academic dishonesty even in the absence of an institutional honor code? The evidence suggests that it will not.

Sierles et al. (1988) examined the effect of the presence or absence of proctors on self-reported cheating on medical school examinations after the school had adopted an honor code. They found more self-reported cheating on the unproctored examinations. Tittle and Rowe (1973) allowed students to grade their own quizzes after the researchers had graded the quizzes without the students' knowledge and found no difference in cheating between students who were reminded that "they were being trusted to grade their quizzes honestly and that they had a moral obligation to be accurate" (p. 489) and those who received no such reminder. Finally, Gardner, Roper, Gonzalez, and Simpson (1988) asked students to sign an honesty pledge for homework assignments halfway through a course. The assignments were structured to facilitate the detection of cheating. They found no difference in cheating rates before and after the pledge or compared to a class whose students had not been asked to make the pledge. In addition, Stern and Havlicek (1986) found that most of the students they surveyed thought that relying on an honor system during exams would probably increase cheating. Thus, course-specific honor systems at best probably have no effect on academic dishonesty and at worst may increase it because some students may interpret the instructor's trust as a license to cheat (e.g., Hollinger & Lanza-Kaduce, 1996).

SUMMARY

In this chapter, we discussed some strategies for fostering academic integrity in and out of the classroom. These strategies include establishing a supportive classroom climate by treating students in ways they perceive to be fair, discussing academic integrity with students, reducing pressure on students, and being available to students outside of class. In the next chapter, we discuss procedures for preventing and detecting academic dishonesty and the problem of how to handle instances of suspected dishonesty.

APPENDIX 3.1: SAMPLE SYLLABUS STATEMENTS

The following are some sample statements for each of the elements discussed in the chapter that you can adapt to your needs. Notice the different tones of the statements that reflect, to a large extent, differences in personality style. Some may seem too weak, some too strong. Say it your way.

When indicated, a statement was taken directly from other campus policies that we thought were well done. As such, they provide ideas that can help you develop your own statement. Most of the statements, however, are ones that we created. Any of these may be used without attribution.

1. An overall statement about the importance of academic integrity in higher education.

a. Academic integrity is central to the mission of this institution. Without honest effort, a learning community has no substance or validity.

b. All students deserve a healthy learning environment and evaluations that are based on their honest, independent efforts. Academic dishonesty pollutes the learning environment.

c. At [name of institution], we also accept the obligation to model and uphold integrity for tomorrow's citizens and leaders. Honesty in all matters academic is an essential requirement of all members of our community.

d. A clear sense of academic honesty and responsibility is fundamental to good scholarship and learning. As members from the academic community, students have final responsibility for conducting themselves is accordance with these expectations. Where a breach of academic honesty is suspected, the university must treat the matter with a level of seriousness that reflects the fundamental importance we attach to academic honesty. At the same time, the university has in place a formal process that protects students' rights. [York University]

e. Academic honesty and integrity are essential to the existence and growth of an academic community. Without maintenance of high standards of honesty, members of the instructional faculty are defrauded, students are unfairly treated, and society is poorly served. [University of North Carolina at Charlotte]

f. Academic dishonesty violates the most fundamental values of an intellectual community and depreciates the achievements of the entire college community. [Babson College]

g. Academic dishonesty is an affront to the integrity of scholarship and a threat to the quality of learning. [University of San Diego]

h. Academic freedom is a fundamental right in any institution of higher learning. Honesty and integrity are necessary preconditions of this freedom. [Rutgers University]

i. Our community of scholars is dedicated to personal and academic excellence. Joining this community obligates each member to observe the principles of mutual respect, academic integrity, civil discourse, and responsible decision making. Academic integrity finds its genesis in the fundamental values of honesty, tolerance, respect, rigor, fairness, and the pursuit of truth. [Lewis and Clark College]

j. Dishonesty hurts us all. It adds suspicion and resentment to academic competition, and it distorts the meaning of grades. If academic dishonesty is widespread or accepted even tacitly, it can undermine and demoralize our common efforts. [Duke University]

k. Honesty, trust, and personal responsibility are fundamental attributes of the university community. Academic dishonesty threatens the foundation of an institution dedicated to the pursuit of knowledge. To maintain its credibility and reputation, and to equitably assign evaluations of scholastic and creative performance, [name of school] is committed to maintaining a climate that upholds and values the highest standards of academic integrity. [Ball State University]

2. A personal statement declaring your commitment to academic honesty.

a. I am strongly committed to assigning grades based on my students' honest efforts on exams and other class assignments. I am strongly committed to ensuring that students who do honest work are not disadvantaged by students who cheat. Academic dishonesty in any form, therefore, will not be tolerated in my classes.

b. I am sympathetic to the many pressures that face today's college students. Some students may consider committing acts of academic dishonesty as a way of relieving those pressures. This is not a legitimate solution; I can neither condone nor tolerate it. I will give you all the help that I can with this course, and other resources are available on campus to assist you with many of the academic and personal problems you may be facing.

c. To honor students who are here to learn and who take pride in their own work, I will actively pursue any reasonable suspicions or allegations that cheating has occurred.

d. I take an active role in upholding the honesty code [or name of institutional code] of [name of institution]. I will take action on any evidence that cheating may have occurred.

e. I view instances of cheating or plagiarism with great concern and will watch carefully for them.

f. My colleagues and I are committed to the highest standards of academic integrity. In accordance with [institution's] guidelines, we will take vigorous action against students who engage in cheating, plagiarism, forgery, misrepresentation, fraud, or other dishonest practices.

g. All students are expected to maintain the highest standards of academic honesty. There will be no excuses accepted for plagiarism, cheating, or any other act that suggests you have not fulfilled your academic responsibilities in this course.

3. *How you will deal with any incidents that you observe or that come to your attention.*

a. I will confront directly students suspected of cheating, although this will normally be done in the privacy of my office.

b. If I observe academic dishonesty or if suspicions of cheating are reported to me by my teaching assistant or other students, I will request the identified parties to come to my office to discuss the allegation and discuss what will happen next.

c. Confronting students who are under suspicion for cheating is onerous and anxiety arousing, even for professors. However, because I am committed to upholding our honesty policy, I will call into my office any student who has given me (or others who report to me) reason to suspect a possible violation of our school policy.

d. All suspected incidents of academic dishonesty will be vigorously pursued.

e. If you cheat on homework or an exam, you will receive a grade of zero on that assignment. If you cheat a second time, I will seek to fail you in the course. [*Note:* Your school's policy may not allow you to fail a student on your own. Hence, the wording "seek to."]

f. I hold every student responsible for knowing the honesty policy at [name of institution]. The policy can be found [give information].

Ignorance or misunderstanding of the honesty policy will not serve as an excuse for academic dishonesty.

g. Any instance of alleged or suspected academic dishonesty will be processed through the established channels.

4. *A brief list of the types of academic dishonesty in your school's policy (with reference to where the complete policy can be found) and a brief comment about the range of penalties.* This list needs to be generated from your institution's own academic dishonesty policy. Some policies are very brief, listing disallowed behaviors by name only. Others offer elaborate definitions. The ideal syllabus statement contains at least the list and possibly very brief definitions (or examples of how such acts might reveals themselves in your classes).

a. Acts of academic dishonesty include cheating on exams (such as using unauthorized notes or looking at a neighbor's paper), plagiarism (copying the work of others and claiming them as your own), facilitation (helping another cheat), unauthorized collaboration (working with others when independent effort was specifically assigned), [and so on]. The code at [name of institution] allows disciplinary sanctions that range from assignment of a zero on the assignment to expulsion from the [college or university].

b. I fully support the college academic honesty policy. Acts of dishonesty include. . . . I act in accordance with the procedures for handling acts of academic dishonesty. The formal procedure involves a judiciary committee composing faculty and students. Penalties include assigning students to an integrity seminar, lowering or failing grades on an assignment or in the course, and suspending or expelling them from the college. The complete honesty policy and the procedure for processing students accused of dishonesty can be found in the Student Handbook and on the campus web site under Student Rights and Responsibilities.

5. *A brief list of any types of academic dishonesty that could occur in your particular course and that would benefit from offering more detail.* Despite a single all-campus policy, instructors do differ in the emphases and seriousness with which they pursue academic dishonesty. Therefore, it is wise to be clear about types of dishonesty and the form they would take in your classes. It is especially important to define the boundaries of authorized collaboration with other students. It also helps if you briefly justify why independent

effort is important (see 5-b). The following are some examples of how these statements might look.

a. Although less often discussed, oral plagiarism is a form of academic dishonesty. Therefore, as you are compiling your oral report assignment, be sure that you "find your own voice." Generally, the same rules apply as for written plagiarism. Although you are not required to state the entire bibliographic reference list, do give brief credit in your verbal report to any directly quoted or paraphrased materials. If your words are inspired by the work of another, even though you neither copied nor paraphrased, it is appropriate to give that source brief credit as well. Please list complete bibliographic information in the written version of your oral report that you turn into me.

b. This class requires many take-home assignments. It is expected that you will do your problems independently and will not collaborate with or copy answers from others. If you are having trouble with your problem sets, you can see me and I will try to help you get back on track. It is important to do your own work because you will not learn the process unless you learn to cope with each phase on your own. You will have great difficulty performing well on exams unless you have fully mastered and understand the steps.

c. Occasional incidents involving sabotage of laboratory specimens have been reported. This is a serious form of academic dishonesty. Any student who alters, defiles, or exchanges the dogfish shark specimen of another student or students will be dealt with to the fullest extent of our academic honesty policy.

d. This is a very large class and the seats are bolted to the floor. To avoid coming under suspicion during examinations, be sure to keep your eyes on your own papers.

6. *List of campus resources that may help reduce the risk factors associated with cheating.* Some common risk factors associated with cheating that can be addressed by campus resources include poor study habits, poor writing skills or inadequate training in how to prepare written assignments, procrastination, stress or depression, poor time management skills, weak refusal skills, feelings of alienation, too-high course loads, test anxiety, and fear of failure. Most campuses offer some form of assistance for students at risk, most commonly learning, tutoring, advisement, and counseling services. Including basic information about these resources in a syllabus also provides a

good opportunity to offer a booster statement that helps diffuse any perceived stigma associated with seeking help.

a. Many factors that put students at risk for cheating can be prevented. This campus has programs designed to help you before problems get out of hand. If you have difficulties with procrastination or study techniques, the Learning Center offers pamphlets and brief seminars about techniques that can be effective for overcoming study blocks and getting the most out of study time. If you have personal difficulties (such as depression or relationship problems) that are interfering with your studies, the counselors at the Student Counseling Center specialize in helping students with the kinds of problems that students may face.

b. To do your best work, you may need to take advantage of some of the resources on campus. These include the study tables in the library (8 a.m. to 10 p.m. every week day) , the peer-tutoring program in the student center (by appointment), and the Counseling Center (Administration building, by appointment). I have checked out all of these resources myself and highly recommend them to any student.

c. Need additional help with how to cite information in your papers? Check out our web page under "Proper Ways to Cite Sources" in the "Student Support Resources" section. This page has other resources on campus that can help you with anything from career counseling to what to do in a medical emergency. The site is very cleverly done, and I highly recommend it.

7. *An invitation to approach you directly to discuss anything that is unclear or confusing regarding academic dishonesty.* Many students are reluctant to show any ignorance and may be especially intimidated at the thought of openly discussing a behavior that might be dishonest. However, a welcoming invitation that acknowledges the existence of confusion and misunderstandings may save you and the student from later being ensnared in more agonizing interactions.

a. Sometimes the rules regarding academic integrity can be confusing when you apply them to the work you are doing in my class. Sometimes students do not understand the assignment and may unwittingly commit an act of academic dishonesty. However, ignorance will not be a valid excuse. If you have questions, please come see me. I am always willing to help a student avoid any misunderstanding or mistakes that could carry long-term, negative consequences.

b. If you have any questions or are confused about appropriate and inappropriate use of resources, I am available to help clarify the matter. If you have not had much experience in writing the kinds of assignments required in this course, I highly recommend that you visit the learning center and sign up for a writing tutor or one of the workshops that are given starting next week.

c. You are always welcome to stop by during office hours or after class for a fuller explanation of anything pertaining to this course. This includes any clarifications needed regarding academic dishonesty.

8. *An invitation to report incidents of academic dishonesty.* Most students have observed academic dishonesty among their peers, but few will report it. However, a written invitation may, in and of itself, have a salutary effect. Students know that a single professor (or a professor and one teaching assistant) cannot see everything that goes on, especially in large classes. However, if a student who is considering cheating knows that anyone in the room might report his or her dishonest behavior, an impulse to cheat might be reconsidered.

a. Students are usually reluctant to report cheating incidents. However, I encourage you to tell me if you observe cheating. I will not use your name unless you give me permission. However, it is helpful to me to be alerted to any problems that I do not observe myself.

b. I invite you to approach me in private with any concerns you have about a classmate's behavior. I will hold your comments confidential unless you give me permission to identify you.

c. If you directly observe any student engaging in any form of academic dishonesty, I hope you will make an appointment to come and tell me about it.

d. This course is graded on a curve. That means that students who cheat could bump your grade down. That bothers me and it should bother you, too. I hope that you will report to me any directly observed act of academic dishonesty.

A cautionary note: *Ensure that your syllabus statements do not contradict the all-school policy.* Instances have been reported involving instructors who apparently believed that scary threats would deter cheating. As an example: *"If I even suspect that you are cheating, you will be expelled from this institution."* This statement was at startling variance with the institution's policy, which included the necessary provisions for a lengthy procedure requiring due process for any extreme penalty.

APPENDIX 3.2: TEACHING STUDENTS
ABOUT PLAGIARISM

This appendix presents some ideas for teaching students about plagiarism, adapted from the *Copy Cats* segment of the Multimedia Integrity Teaching Tool (Keith-Spiegel, 1999). The information presented here is based on original script materials written by Keith-Spiegel, general knowledge, and questions and comments from nine focus groups conducted with undergraduate students.

I. WHY PLAGIARISM IS A PROBLEM

Plagiarism is WRONG because it involves:

- a misrepresentation of yourself
- stealing what belongs to others
- a violation of your school's academic honesty policy
- a violation of copyright law
- dishonoring and undermining your classmates who do their own work
- deceiving your instructors
- interfering with real learning

II. TYPES OF PLAGIARISM

A. *Overall definition:* Plagiarism is the undocumented use of the work or concepts created by others. Plagiarists claim the work of others as their own or do not fully or appropriately credit their sources. Although plagiarism is usually discussed with regards to writings, the concept of *work* can be extended to include other forms of expression such as musical compositions, designs, and speeches.

B. *The four major types of plagiarism*

TYPE 1: *Direct Plagiarism:* A written work is copied word for word from another source and submitted as if you conceived of this word pattern yourself. Even if phrases are slightly modified, you would still be committing direct plagiarism. Consider the following example:

The Original Author's Passage: The college experience raises confidence at the same time it nourishes insecurity. It expands social circles and fosters isolation. It fosters goal seeking and the value of the moment. It forces both good and bad decisions. By its end, maturity is closer at hand.

The Student's Version (Original words in italics): College life increases self-*confidence and nourishes insecurity. It* also *expands social* life but *fosters isolation* at the same time. *It fosters goal seeking* as well as *the values of the moment. It forces both good and bad decisions. Maturity* is the result.

Comment: The student does not use all of the original author's words, but the student's own words are little more than an alternative way to connect the original author's basic content. Nothing original or reflective of the student's own process emerges here.

Direct plagiarism could have been avoided had the student quoted the passage or put quote marks around the borrowed words, and also credited the passage to the original author. The borrowed text also could have been paraphrased and attributed to the original author in a footnote or other appropriate citation method.

TYPE 2: *Unattributed Paraphrasing:* In unattributed paraphrasing, the writer may actually use few or no words from the original source. However, the writer's version is heavily dependent on the source and contains no new concepts or perspectives. The author of the original source, however, is given no credit. Consider the following example:

> *The Original Author's Passage:* How can anyone say that rejection is as easy to sluff off as yesterday's leftovers? Rejection carries with it a pain so piercing that one might as well have taken a harpoon in the heart. With time the pain softens, but a permanent scar scores the soul. The fortunate ones learn something, managing to carry fewer marks.

> *The Student's Version:* Can you doubt that rejection experiences can be dismissed like yesterday's meat loaf? Rejection is as painful as being stabbed with a knife. The wound eventually heals but leaves a mark on one's soul. Some people learn from rejection experiences. They are the lucky ones.

> *Comment:* The paraphrased version is too close to the original, despite very little word overlap, to be submitted as original work. Plagiarism could have been easily avoided by appropriately crediting the original author (in a footnote or other citation method).

TYPE 3: *Insufficient Citation of Sources:* If sources are not *appropriately* credited, plagiarism can be the intentional (or unintentional) result. Proper citations are sufficiently complete to allow the reader to locate and consult that source. Because there are several citation methods, check with your instructor if you are confused about which one to use. In some types of writing, such as journalism, citations are less detailed because of the nature of the work products.

TYPE 4: *Pirating Distinctive Concepts:* Claiming as one's own the distinctive concepts, ideas, or approaches to a subject developed by others constitutes plagiarism. Consider the following example:

The Original Author's Passage: We must rethink how we teach values to our young. Children are self-centered and lack the capacity to experience abstract rewards. Rather than attempting to convince children that goodness is the right way to be, we should reward them directly for being good. In short, let kids know what's in it for them.

The Student's (Unattributed) Adaptation: Nightly news stories regularly feature children who commit crimes. The older members of my family have observed that the younger kids show less respect to others than they did in my generation. I propose that we devise a scheme that directly rewards children when they behave. After all, children are self-absorbed and cannot easily relate to abstract concepts such as "rightness."

Comment: Although the student's statement contains some original observations and there is no direct copying of words, an idea was heavily borrowed but not credited to the original author. This passage would have been acceptable had the original author been cited as the source of the idea. The student would then be free to adapt or expand on the premise.

III. RED FLAGS: SIGNS THAT PLAGIARISM COULD OCCUR

• *Waiting too long before starting a writing assignment.* The longer students wait to start working on a writing assignment, the greater the temptation to plagiarize. Even if students do not intend to cheat, they may commit some form of plagiarism without even realizing it. Haste and panic are breeding grounds for sloppy scholarship, inadequate citations, and unintentional copying.

• *Underestimating what it means to be a college student.* College standards for original scholarship are much higher, and tolerance for plagiarism is much lower, than was true in high school. Students who got by with unattributed paraphrasing in high school may be unprepared for the serious consequences of these same acts in college.

• *Generalizing from less strict instructors.* Some instructors are not as watchful as others, and plagiarism is not always easy to identify. However, it is very unwise to conclude that plagiarism will go undetected. Many instructors are *very* vigilant and will go to great lengths to detect plagiarism. Remember that instructors are experts in the areas they teach. They may know immediately where any plagiarized passages originated.

• *Generalizing from one discipline to another.* Every department expects writing assignments to be based on the original and independent efforts of their students. However, the emphasis put on the type and completeness of citations vary somewhat from one discipline to another. It is important to realize that these differences exist and to play it safe by always citing your sources carefully.

• *Taking sloppy research notes.* Plagiarism can occur inadvertently by copying notes directly from a source and forgetting that the notes are the same, word-for-word, as the original course. However, students are still responsible for this mistake. As you are taking notes, be sure that you put quote marks (and the page number) around everything that you copy directly. Careful documentation during your search for sources will ensure correct citations later.

• *Establishing a VERY bad habit.* Committing all forms of plagiarism can become a bad habit (often one that started well before college). Successful careers have been destroyed when instances of plagiarism come to light years later.

IV. ANSWERS TO QUESTIONS STUDENTS OFTEN ASK

• *I get overwhelmed with writing assignments. Where do I start?* Some students plagiarize—purposely, unintentionally, or both—because they have never learned how to research information and build on or integrate it into their own writing process. Most college instructors simply assume that students already know how to write a paper and cite references properly. If you are overwhelmed, seek out opportunities on your campus to improve your research and writing skills *as soon as possible.* Your instructor can direct you to sources of advice and assistance.

• *Won't my instructors think that I am stupid if I haven't learned how to write a paper by the time I get to college?* It is always acceptable to ask for help. It is better to feel a little embarrassed than to be accused of plagiarism. Remember that you are *not* the only one who hasn't mastered writing skills. Resources exist on your campus to help ensure that you are writing and citing resources appropriately. These include English instructors, librarians, writing laboratories, tutors, and helpful books on the subject.

• *Hey, students make mistakes. I don't see why plagiarism is such a big deal while we are still in school.* Expectations for responsible scholarship and integrity are higher than they have been before. Mistakes are no longer discounted as due to mere immaturity.

• *What if I just don't like writing papers?* Some students choose to plagiarize because they do not like to write. But that is *not* an excuse to commit academic fraud. Try to keep in mind that the thinking and communication skills you are practicing will serve you well in whatever life endeavor you choose.

• *It seems to me that my professors do not agree when it comes to how to cite sources. Why is this so confusing?* Your instructors may differ in their expectations of how you cite sources and other aspects of writing requirements. Make sure that you understand *exactly* what *each* instructor expects. If you are confused by the syllabus or the directions that were given in class, talk to your instructor. It is each instructor's obligation to make sure his or her students have a clear understanding of course assignments. Instructors may not know that you need help unless you ask them for it.

• *Isn't some information simply common knowledge that doesn't require any citation?* Common knowledge refers to general information in the public domain that is widely used. Often the particular originator is not known. Frequently heard sayings (such as, "An ounce of prevention is worth a pound of cure") and the names of state capitols are examples of common knowledge. The problem is that students may not always be aware of where the line is drawn between common knowledge and material that must be cited. When in doubt, cite! Crediting the sources that helped you create your paper is always proper (and safe).

• *Doesn't the instructor assume that you can't think for yourself if you use a lot of citations?* College instructors may not likely assign you a good grade if all you do is link quotes together. But when you use the ideas and works of others to build on as you develop your own ideas and interpretations, instructors will be impressed with your extensive research. That is how good scholarship is done.

• *If you use material that is not from a book or other publication, do you have to cite it?* Even if someone else's work is not published in print or copyrighted, claiming it as one's own is *still* plagiarism. For example, failing to document material accessed from the Internet is considered plagiarism.

• *Isn't it possible for a student to independently create an idea or concept without any awareness that someone else had already done it?* Yes, this can happen. Sometimes students are put in the position of having to convince their instructors that their notions were derived without access to similar preexisting work. But, many concepts and ideas are so distinctive that the chances of duplication are low.

• *Is it better to use direct quotes than to paraphrase?* Not necessarily. Quotes are best used whenever the exact words enhance your presentation. Properly cited paraphrased material, however, is often more appropriate because it allows you to shorten or simplify the original work as you weave it into your own content and style.

V. HOW PLAGIARISM CHEATS YOU. (These reasons were student-generated.)

• You learn nothing when you copy an assignment.
• You miss out on opportunities to master research and writing skills—two essential abilities in today's marketplace.
• You do not experience the gratification that comes from creating something that is distinctly your own.
• If you commit plagiarism and it is discovered, your career is ruined before it starts.
• You let yourself down.

4

Preventing and Detecting Academic Dishonesty

◆ ◆ ◆

Techniques for fostering academic integrity, such as those presented in the last chapter, are effective with some students. Other students remain unaffected. As noted in chapter 2, student attitudes are a major factor influencing academic dishonesty; students who see academic dishonesty as a legitimate means of achieving their goals are likely to engage in dishonest behavior regardless of the classroom atmosphere. As a respondent to a survey conducted by one of us put it, "Anything worth having is worth cheating for." Consequently, academic dishonesty is likely to be a problem unless instructors utilize measures to prevent and detect it.

This chapter presents some suggestions, drawn from a variety of sources, for preventing and detecting cheating. We discuss two techniques: discussion of academic integrity issues and increasing the likelihood that students who cheat will be caught. We follow with suggestions for preventing and detecting academic dishonesty on three common categories of academic exercises: homework and lab reports, term papers, and tests. We also discuss students' role in preventing and detecting academic dishonesty.

We understand that instructors enter their careers to teach and enlighten, not to become exam police—suspicious of students, watching for any sign of dishonest activity. However, we also respect the literature showing that cheating is rampant on most campuses and that both honest students and the academy are victimized by students who cheat. However, we do not intend to imply that all, or even most, students are dishonest. Although academic dishonesty is a problem, we should approach the task of its control with an attitude of vigilance, not one of distrust. Such an approach will not only help deter dishonest students, but will also reassure honest students that we have their welfare at heart. We ask that you keep this perspective in mind when reviewing the techniques for preventing, detecting, and handling cases of academic dishonesty presented in this chapter and the next.

GENERAL PREVENTION TECHNIQUES

We start with two techniques for preventing academic dishonesty that are unrelated to any particular type of academic exercise: discussions of academic dishonesty and increasing the risk of detection of dishonest behavior.

Discussions of Academic Dishonesty

In chapter 3 we examined discussing academic integrity as a means of fostering integrity. Here we examine the reverse of the coin: discussing academic dishonesty as a means of preventing dishonesty. These discussions can incorporate several elements: discussions of the problem of academic dishonesty, threats of punishment, and moral appeals to students' sense of integrity.

Discussion of the Problem. In his survey of college students, Aiken (1991) found that 55% of his respondents thought that discussing the problem of academic dishonesty would be an effective means to prevent dishonesty. Although Aiken did not ask students what the discussion should consist of, we suggest letting students know that:

- you are aware that cheating and other forms of academic dishonesty take place,
- you understand the various techniques that cheaters use,
- you intend to institute preventive measures,
- cheaters who are detected will be punished or reported, and
- you want to create a climate of trust and mutual respect

Regarding the last point, one should also tell the class that any suspicious behavior during exams will be discussed privately with the students concerned so that other students are not distracted. Otherwise, students who do not see immediate action being taken may assume that the instructor really does not care about cheating. Also, as we discuss later, there are nondisruptive actions that one can take to let students know that the instructor is aware of suspicious behavior and intends to take action.

This kind of discussion not only alerts students to your intention to confront and deal with academic dishonesty, but also that you care about it as a problem. Genereaux and McLeod (1995) found that students believe that academic dishonesty increases when instructors give the impression that students' honesty is unimportant to them.

In our experience, it is helpful to attempt to make a discussion of cheating interactive. Some questions (if relevant to your class) that can open up more assertive students (and others will often follow once the discussion takes off) include:

- How many of you have witnessed another student cheating?
- How did you feel when you saw another student cheating?
- How do students who cheat hurt you?
- Some students may not cheat for themselves, but are willing to help a friend cheat. Can you think of reasons as to why this is not really helping a friend?
- Are the general rules concerning plagiarism unclear? Do you think it is necessary for me to provide additional assistance about avoiding plagiarism to help ensure that the rules are followed for the writing assignments in this class? The same general question can be asked about how to properly attribute the work of others.
- Do you understand my policy regarding unpermitted collaboration? Present some examples of what you would find acceptable and unacceptable. Also ask students to provide examples for you to comment on.
- Do you know how to avoid social loafing and free riding on group assignments? Spelling out the meaning of these undesirable labels may, in and of itself, have a positive impact.
- How do you think we [instructors] feel when we become aware that a student has cheated?

The last question offers an opportunity to describe the hurt, disappointment, anger, and frustration we feel when we have to deal with academic dishonesty. We have found that most students seem both amazed and impressed on learning that instructors take such acts so personally and that they have such strong, negative reactions. This question also opens up the possibility of correcting a common misperception. Students have sometimes seen instructors observe cheating and apparently not do anything about it, and they conclude that instructors do not care about cheating. You can inform students that most instructors do not confront suspected offenders in public to protect the privacy of those students.

Threats of Punishment. Although discussions of academic dishonesty should include information about penalties for violations of academic integrity, threats of punishment are not very effective in forestalling academic dishonesty. Several studies have found that threats or fear of punishment do little to inhibit cheating (Heisler, 1974; Lanza-Kaduce & Klug, 1986; McCabe & Trevino, 1993). It is not clear whether the low effectiveness of threats results from students' beliefs that they will not be caught or from the belief that even if caught they will not be punished or will receive only insignificant punishment. Regardless, a threats-only approach may breed dislike for the instructor, which could possibly motivate cheating.

Moral Appeals. Pavela and McCabe (1993) suggested that faculty and administrators "appeal to the students' sense of honor and personal integrity" as a means of preventing academic dishonesty (p. 28). However, such appeals may be more effective for some students than for others (Gardner et al., 1988; Tittle & Rowe, 1973). For example, Aiken (1991), found that 68% of his sample of students from a private, church-related university thought that such appeals would be effective compared with 38% of his sample from a nearby public university.

Increasing the Risk of Detection

Although many students are willing to engage in academic dishonesty, none want to get caught: Several studies have found that risk of detection inhibits cheating (Houston, 1983; Michaels & Miethe, 1989; Tittle & Rowe, 1973). Therefore, most of the suggestions for preventing academic dishonesty offered in the next three sections focus on instilling in students the belief that the risk of detection is high if they choose to cheat. Nonetheless, a high risk of detection is not sufficient to prevent dishonesty: Students who contemplate cheating tend to weigh the risk of detection and punishment against the benefits they expect to derive from dishonesty and will cheat if they perceive the expected benefits outweigh the potential costs (Michaels & Miethe, 1989).

HOMEWORK ASSIGNMENTS, PROBLEM SETS, AND LAB REPORTS

This and the next two sections on term papers and exams are each divided into two parts: suggestions for preventing academic dishonesty and suggestions for detecting dishonesty.

Prevention

One clear way to prevent a major form of cheating on homework assignments—copying from files kept of old assignments—is to change the questions or exercises each semester or quarter. Although this approach entails considerable work at first, once several sets of questions have been developed, the questions can be reused by creating combinations of questions from different forms. For example, Form E of an assignment could include Question 1 from Form A, Question 2 from Form B, Question 3 from Form C, and Question 4 from Form D. Even having only four alternatives for each of four questions on a homework assignment allows for 24 versions of the assignment.

If you cannot change the contents of an assignment, then you should have students turn in two copies of each assignment, keeping one in your file. This way students know that you have the capability of comparing their work to that turned in by students previously enrolled in the course.

Some types of homework assignments can involve date-sensitive material. For example, if students are asked to report on current events that occurred no longer than a few weeks ago or on articles from recent issues of scholarly journals, reusing old assignments becomes impossible.

Students who copy lab reports from file copies present an especially difficult problem. Lab assignments often cannot be changed much from term to term because they involve standard techniques that all students must follow (Paldy, 1996). In addition, in the physical and biological sciences, at least, every student who correctly carries out an experiment should obtain virtually identical results, thus similarity of results cannot be used as an indicator of cheating. One way to deal with the file copy problem is to closely monitor attendance at labs. This procedure ensures that students are present for the entire lab period and actually carry out the experiment; students who don't attend, who leave early, or who are present but don't do the work have no basis for writing a report and so should not turn one in.

It is important to be explicit about the degree, if any, to which students are allowed to collaborate on assignments and the amount and type of help, if any, they are allowed to receive. As we noted in chapter 3, students are likely to assume that full collaboration and any type of help are authorized unless they are told otherwise. It is also important to inform potential helpers, such as reference librarians and writing tutors, what kinds of help are permitted. For example, reference librarians could be allowed to show students how to use a resource, but not to help them answer a homework question involving the use of the resource. Providing librarians with copies of homework assignments will assist them to avoid giving inappropriate assistance.

Finally, many students prepare homework assignments and lab reports on computers available in public computer labs. It is a good idea to warn students not to store their work on those computers' hard drives or other shared storage devices such as network servers. Other students can gain access to their work, and dishonest students might steal it.

Detection

Do not assume that changing homework questions each semester will prevent copying from files: One of us once had two students in the same class section turn in identically wrong answers to a homework assignment, but those answers were perfectly correct for the previous semester's questions! The students had not bothered checking to see whether the questions had changed before copying from a homework file.

Student copying of answers to written homework assignments from each other can be detected by carefully comparing students' answers: Different students' answers to a question should differ in writing style even when the answer is correct. If you can read all homework assignments in a single sitting, your chances of detecting students who copied directly from each other are substantially heightened. Patterns of similar errors suggest that copying has taken place, although innocent similarities are possible, as when students study together and pass their mistakes on to each other but complete the assignment independently.

You should also be alert for answers that seem to be too good given the student's demonstrated level of ability. Such answers could indicate copying from an instructor's manual if questions from the manual were used, copying from a homework file, or having the assignment done by a more skilled student who had previously taken the course. Copying from homework files can be detected by comparing current submissions with previous submissions, especially when an answer sounds familiar. Although this is a labor-intensive and time-consuming process, it can be effective.

Table 4.1 summarizes some suggestions for preventing and detecting cheating on homework assignments and lab reports.

TERM PAPERS

Prevention

As with homework assignments and lab reports, one way to prevent students from turning others' work in as their own is to require submission of two copies of the paper so students know that you can check their submissions against previously submitted papers. You can also forestall this

TABLE 4.1
Techniques for Preventing and Detecting Academic
Dishonesty: Homework and Lab Reports

Form of Dishonesty	Prevention	Detection
General	Count as only a small proportion of the final grade Tell students that you keep copies of submissions Monitor attendance at lab sessions: Students who don't attend cannot do the work on which to write the report	Retain copies of submissions
Copying answers from instructor's manual	Do not use questions from the instructor's manual	Compare submissions with the instructor's manual Watch for answers that are *too good*
Copying answers from other students	Be explicit about the degree of collaboration, if any, allowed Watch for patterns of error similarity Monitor lab attendance Warn students against storing work on multiple-user computer devices such as shared computers	Compare students' answers
Copying answers from earlier terms assignments	Change questions frequently	Watch for errors that were correct answers in earlier terms
Receiving unauthorized assistance	Be explicit about who can give assistance and what kinds of assistance are permitted Inform potential helpers (e.g., librarians) about limits on assistance	Watch for answers that are *too good*

Note. Adapted from A. C. Singhal & P. Johnson, "How to Halt Student Dishonesty, *College Student Journal,* 1983, *17,* pp. 13–19. Adapted with permission of *College Student Journal*, P.O. Box 8508, Spring Hill Station, Mobile, AL 36689–9508 problem by specifying the topics about which students can write (changing the topics frequently) and allowing no last-minute changes to the paper.

Narrowly or very specifically defining the term paper assignment makes plagiarism more difficult or at least more difficult for plagiarism to enhance the student's grade. It is less likely that a student can locate "just the right paper" on the Web or elsewhere if the assignment is very specific about the required approach to the topic and the manner in which the term paper is to be organized.

Another way to help ensure that students are doing their own work is to have them provide information about the paper as they write it, for example by having them first submit a bibliography, then an outline, and then a draft, and requiring substantial changes between the draft and the final paper. This procedure has the additional benefit that the feedback you provide at each stage should help the students write better papers. You can also explain the procedure to students in terms of writing improvement rather than cheating prevention. Although pedagogically sound, this procedure is very labor intensive and is unlikely to be practical for large classes unless the instructor has considerable assistance.

One can also verify that the work is the students' own by checking their knowledge of the contents by giving pop quizzes or requiring brief oral reports on their topics. The latter procedure has the pedagogical benefit of helping students learn how to present concise verbal summaries of their written work—a task that many will have to perform as part of their postcollege careers. The syllabus should inform students that they might be asked to discuss their papers with the instructor so that they understand from the outset that they are accountable for what they write.

As Roig (1997, 1999) has shown, plagiarism often stems from students' ignorance of how to avoid it rather than from dishonesty (see chapt. 3). Consequently, one way to prevent this problem is to ensure that students have the necessary skills, such as how to paraphrase text properly and how to cite sources properly. Also, students may not be aware that it is improper to turn the same paper in for credit in more than one course without the instructor's permission; be sure to clearly explain your policy on this matter.

Another problem that can occur with term papers is fabricated bibliography items, especially if you require a minimum number of items. One suggestion is to require students to turn in photocopies of the title pages of the books and the first pages of the journal articles they cited. Although some students might be tempted simply to copy the pages without actually reading the sources, notifying students that they might be required to discuss their sources with the instructor, and actually having some do so, may deter them from citing unread sources.

Finally, many students prepare papers on computers available in public computer labs. As is the case with homework assignments and lab reports, it is a good idea to warn students not to store their work on those computers' hard drives or other shared storage devices such as network servers. Other students can gain access to their work, and dishonest students might steal all or parts of it.

Detection

Papers purchased from term paper mills or copied directly from sources often stand out because the work appears to be too professionally written. Therefore, it can be useful to compare term papers with examples of students' in-class writing, such as brief essays written during class and responses to essay or short-answer questions on exams. Similarly, plagiarized passages within a paper stand out because of the difference in writing style between the student and the author of the copied text. One way to check such passages is to require students to turn in complete copies of all sources used or of the relevant sections of lengthy sources, such as books. This is not an arduous requirement for papers for which only a few sources are required. Students often copy them for their own use anyway.

We should note that some term paper mills, especially sites on the World Wide Web that do not charge for papers, provide papers (often of marginal quality) written by students with grammatical, spelling, and other errors left uncorrected. These acts of plagiarism are difficult to detect because they accurately reflect the way many students write. However, if you design the assignment narrowly in terms of expected content and design, large differences between the requirements for the paper and the paper as written may be indications that the student is submitting a bogus paper.

If you suspect that a paper, or a portion of a paper, was downloaded from the Internet, you can use a search engine to find web pages that contain key words and phrases that appear in the suspect work (Benning, 1998). Some online entrepreneurs have also started a fee-based service for identifying sources of papers that might have been plagiarized (Guernsey, 1998).

Finally, keep a file of old term papers indexed by topic to help detect reuse of papers; an index can easily be constructed and maintained as a computerized database file. Such a database could even be maintained for an entire department. Check randomly selected or suspicious papers against file copies of papers on the same topic. Table 4.2 summarizes our suggestions for preventing and detecting cheating on term papers.

EXAMINATIONS

Perhaps more has been written about the prevention of cheating on exams than about the prevention of any other form of academic dishonesty. Cizek (1999) provided an excellent summary of that literature. Therefore, we have divided our discussion of prevention measures into three sections: test preparation, test administration, and posttest considerations.

Prevention: Test Preparation

It is difficult for instructors to imagine that their own students would steal from them, but stringent test security procedures are essential as illustrated by the story in Box 4.1. Students sometimes attempt to acquire a copy of an exam prior to its administration. Copies of exams should always be kept under lock and key. If copies are kept in the form of computer files, the files should be on diskettes that are securely stored and not on the hard drives of office computers. If possible, exams should not be duplicated by student employees who might be pressured by friends to provide a copy of the exam. Spoiled copies should be shredded immediately or kept secure until they can be destroyed.

Prevention: Test Administration

There are a number of techniques that can be used during test administration to inhibit cheating. The research on the effectiveness of these techniques is reviewed by Cizek (1999) and Whitley (1998).

Proctoring. The two most common forms of cheating during tests are the use of crib notes and copying from other students. Both of these behaviors can be discouraged by careful proctoring of the exam by the instructor and, if available, teaching assistants. Students do not want to get caught cheating and view proctoring as an effective deterrent (Aiken, 1991; Genereaux & McLeod, 1995; Hollinger & Lanza-Kaduce, 1996; Stern & Havlicek, 1986). Having proctors move around the exam room and proctoring from the back of the room can be especially effective because potential cheaters might reveal themselves by looking around to locate the proctors. The proctors can then give those students special attention. The

TABLE 4.2
Techniques for Preventing and Detecting Academic
Dishonesty: Term Papers

Form of Dishonesty	Prevention	Detection
General	Tell students that you keep copies of old term papers and index them by topic	Retain copies of old term papers
	Give students a set of topics from which to choose and change topics frequently	
	Do not allow last-minute topic changes	
	Require students to submit copies of research notes	
	Require students to submit bibliographies, outlines, and drafts	
	Require substantial changes between drafts and the final paper	
	Require precise formatting criteria for papers; reject those with even slight deviations	
	Give a pop quiz on paper contents	
	Require oral report in addition to paper	
	Warn students against storing work on multiple-user computer devices such as shared computers	

necessity for continual proctoring is illustrated by the note reproduced in Box 4.2, which was found on the floor after an exam during which the instructor left the room for a few minutes to get a drink of water.

Crib Notes. One way to handle the problem of crib notes is to allow students to bring a limited set of notes (e.g., one page or a 3 x 5 card) to the

TABLE 4.2 (continued)

Form of Dishonesty	Prevention	Detection
Plagiarism	Teach students how to paraphrase and cite sources properly	Watch for phrasing that is too professional Watch for fluctuations in writing style Compare papers with in-class writing assignments Require students to turn in copies of sources Search the Internet for suspicious key phrases
Faking bibliography items	Require students to turn in copies of title pages of books and first pages of cited articles	
Buying from term paper mills	Let students know that you're aware of the problem	Watch for papers that are *too good*

Note. Adapted from A. C. Singhal & P. Johnson, "How to Halt Student Dishonesty, *College Student Journal*, 1983, *17*, pp. 13–19. Adapted with permission of *College Student Journal*, P.O. Box 8508, Spring Hill Station, Mobile, AL 36689–9508.

test. Although at first glance this strategy might seem to render the test moot, research has shown that, on the average, students who are allowed to use notes during exams perform no better than students who are not allowed notes (e.g., Whitley, 1996). There is a potential negative side effect to this technique—namely, that some students may study less, thinking that they do not need to actually know and understand the material.

If you do not want to allow students to use notes, there are several steps that can be taken to inhibit the use of crib notes:

1. Put an explicit statement in your syllabus concerning what materials students may and may not use during exams, and reinforce your policy with oral instructions prior to the test.

BOX 4.1
Stealing Examinations

It is upsetting to think that our own students, whom we tend to both like and trust, would enter into our private domains to steal a copy of an examination. But it does happen. We helped advise two colleagues in our own medium-size department within the last 2 years. In both cases, the theft took place in a matter of seconds while the instructors left their offices open to attend to personal needs. In both cases, the discovery was as much due to luck as anything else. In the first instance, the instructor had already numbered the exams sequentially. He noticed prior to giving the exam that Number 31 was missing because, as he put it, "I just happened to be thumbing through the stack while on the phone." In the second instance, an informant told the instructor that she overheard two students discussing the theft of the exam.

2. If the lay-out of the exam room permits, require students to leave books, coats, backpacks, and other carry-in items at the back or front of the room during the test.

3. Sports caps are very popular, but ask that students not wear them (or other brimmed hats) during the test. Ask students who forget and wear them anyway to turn the brim around to the back. Brimmed hats facilitate cheating in two ways: Notes can be written on the underside of the brim, and it is difficult to detect glances at neighbors' papers.

4. Provide all paper or exam booklets that students will use during the test so that crib notes cannot be hidden in student-supplied test materials.

5. If students bring their own materials (e.g., blue books), collect them a class period or two before the test, check them and mark them with a code so that you know that they've been checked, and randomly redistribute them on exam day.

6. If scratch paper is needed for a test, attach the paper to the test so that students cannot claim that any loose sheets they have are scratch paper.

7. If students are allowed to leave the room during the test, require them to leave their test materials with a proctor. Although this technique will not make it impossible for students to consult crib notes or other materials stowed outside the room, it will make it a little more difficult for them to remember the questions they want to look up and any answers they get from hidden materials. We suggest informing students before the exam is passed

BOX 4.2
A Note off the Classroom Floor: No Comment Necessary

> *Hello dear! I am in my history class. Just finished a killer test. I hope I did well. The professor left the room for a few so it gave us all a chance to cheat. I sure hope it payed off! See you after dinner.*

out to go to the bathroom or sharpen pencils at that time. This may help deter the implementation of premeditated dishonest intentions.

8. Modern technology—in the form of hand-held computers, programmable calculators, and so forth—has provided students with the ability to compile electronic crib notes (Goldsmith, 1998). Gadgets that are (or look like) watches or pens can be programmed to hold considerable amounts of information. You might move in for a closer look at students who seem to be spending an inordinate amount of time looking at their watches or pens! The future may require far more intrusive discovery techniques that ones we envision at this time. Therefore, we recommend that instructors ban all electronic devices except for any that are absolutely required for completion of the exams.

9. Immediately prior to distributing the exams, remind students that you and the other proctors (if they are available) will be watching for cheating and that cheaters will be punished.

Copying. There are a number of steps one can take to reduce the amount of copying from neighbors' exams:

1. The easiest way to inhibit students from copying from others is to spread them out, leaving an empty chair between students in each row and

an empty row between rows with students in them. Students perceive this technique to be an effective deterrent to cheating (Aiken, 1991; Genereaux & McLeod, 1995; Stern & Havlicek, 1986).

2. Because students prefer to copy from friends with whom they have made prior arrangements (Houston, 1986a, 1986b), randomly assigning students to seats for exams could be helpful. However, students generally do not view this technique as effective (Hollinger & Lanza-Kaduce, 1996), so it might not have an inhibitory effect.

3. If manipulation of seating is not practical, as it often is not, multiple test forms should be used, with each student having a different form than the students seated in the adjacent seats and the seats in front and behind. Students who cannot copy from the persons beside them will try to look over the shoulder of the person in front, especially in an auditorium-style room with each row higher than the one in front (Houston, 1976). If it is difficult to achieve such a checkerboard pattern, as it may be in very large classes, we recommend using three or four forms of the test. Alternate test forms can consist either of different sets of items or one set of items in a different order on each form.

If different items are used on each form, scores and grades should be computed within form to avoid the problem of grades being affected by one form being more difficult than the other. Although there may be some concern that scrambling test items to construct different forms might result in different levels of student performance on the different forms (e.g., Gronlund, 1993), research has found that performance is unaffected by item order (Bresnock, Graves, & White, 1989; Gohmann & Spector, 1989). When multiple-choice questions are used, it is also useful to scramble the response options provided for the questions; such scrambling also has no effect on performance (Bresnock et al., 1989).

Make it difficult for students to easily distinguish among forms. One colleague told us how he used two forms of the test, but had one with a blue cover sheet and the other with a yellow cover sheet so that he could quickly sort them for scoring purposes. He seemed to be unaware that students could also make such discriminations, allowing those with dishonest intentions to proceed accordingly.

Students see the use of multiple test forms as an effective deterrent to cheating (Aiken, 1991; Hollinger & Lanza-Kaduce, 1996; Stern & Havlicek, 1986). Thus, informing students during the class period before the exam that multiple forms will be used might discourage some students from conspiring to copy from one another. One could also consider the use of essay questions rather than multiple-choice questions because it is more difficult to copy a narrative than an answer selection. However, there is less agreement among students on the effectiveness of essay questions as a cheating deterrent than there is for multiple test forms (Aiken, 1991; Genereaux & McLeod, 1995; Hollinger & Lanza-Kaduce, 1996; Stern & Havlicek, 1986), and some research suggests that the use of essay questions does little to inhibit cheating (Kerkvliet & Sigmund, 1999).

4. Copying can also be inhibited by requiring students to keep their answers covered. Collaboration can be reduced by forbidding students to share pencils, erasers, and so forth during the exam. Information written on pencils, pens, erasures, and even facial tissues has been confiscated.

5. Finally, do not hesitate to require students to move if you suspect collaboration. Inform students prior to the exam that failing to abide by these rules after one warning will be considered evidence of cheating.

6. As in the case of crib notes, modern technology can facilitate collaboration between students during exams. Devices such as cellular telephones and wireless modems allow students to communicate with collaborators both inside and outside the examination room (Goldsmith, 1998). Once again, a clear ban on the use of such devices during exams can alleviate the problem.

Other Forms of Cheating. Other problems can arise during exams. Students may attempt to take their copies of an exam with them when they finish to add to exam files. This can be forestalled by numbering all exams, assigning exam numbers to students, and ensuring that all are returned. Rarely, more complicated ploys may be attempted, as described in Box 4.3.

Students have also been known to send in more knowledgeable substitutes to take the exam for them. Such ringers can be detected by checking students' identification as they enter the room or turn in the exam. If this is not feasible, you may announce in advance (or in your syllabus) that you or your assistant may spot check identification cards. (You might actually want to do this when a student's face is entirely unfamiliar.) If you have a handwriting sample on all of your students (which can be gathered on the first day of class for an information sheet), you can compare any suspicious test paper. For electronic score sheets, a required signature may be enough to tell the difference between your student and an impostor.

On occasion, students may plan a system of exam answering for in-class assistance (Cizek, 1999). Sound (e.g., pencil tapping, nose sniffing or blowing, coughing) and visual (using fingers or the four corners of the desk)

BOX 4.3
The Complicated Plot to Steal a Test on Exam Day

A colleague told us about an elaborate student plan to abscond with an exam from a large classroom. A small disturbance was created by one student in one part of the room. While all eyes were on the disruptive student, another student on the other side of the room quietly left the room by the back door carrying a copy of the exam. The professor noticed the exiting student and took off after him. Although the instructor never caught the two—who had, by then, joined up just outside the classroom door and taken off running—he did alter the exam (including the makeup for that particular class) substantially, rendering the ploy ineffective.

systems have been identified. It seems to us that these tactics can be easily discovered and squashed by any instructor who is aware of their potential use.

Prevention: After the Test

As noted in chapter 2, many students do not consider getting information about a test from students who took it earlier to be a form of cheating, and so they probably feel free to share such information. Some students may try to write down or memorize questions to pass on to other students who will take the same exam later in the day, the next semester, or as a makeup exam. An effective way to deal with this problem is to use different test questions for each administration of an exam. Letting students know that a make-up exam will consist of different questions may also reduce the number of requests for makeups. Because constructing an alternate objective exam is tedious, one technique that may save instructors' time in the long run is to rewrite some new multiple-choice questions and delete a number of others, or to substitute short answer or essay questions, using items that are easy to grade, for some multiple-choice questions. Although students taking makeup exams may derive some advantage from information passed on by other students, it is not likely to be enough to get a high score.

If you return tests and scored answer sheets or booklets for the purpose of reviewing the questions and correct answers with students, have students put their names on the tests at the time of the exam and give students their own exams as well as their answer sheets or booklets (stapled all together if appropriate). Then check to ensure that all are returned; if any are missing, you will know whose they were.

Several steps can be taken to prevent students from changing answers and then claiming a scoring error. One is to copy machine-scored answer sheets before returning them and letting students know in advance that you do so. When multiple-choice exams are hand scored, mark the correct answer in red ink so students cannot write over it. Similarly, mark out any blank space left at the end of a short answer or essay question, and write "not answered" in the space left on the answer sheet or booklet for the responses to omitted questions.

Finally, keep tests locked up *after* administration as well as before to prevent them from wandering. When tests are no longer needed, shred them or otherwise permanently destroy them so they cannot be recovered from the trash.

Detection

As with the prevention of cheating, careful proctoring of exams is probably the best means to detect cheating. Watch for any off-task, unusual, or suspicious behavior, such as students' looking in their laps for crib notes, extraneous paper on which notes might be written, and the wandering eyes syndrome for copying. Having a proctor stand near the possible offender will usually prevent further attempts. The use of crib notes on essay or short answer exams may sometimes be indicated by answers that sound too good to be written by a student, especially under the pressure of an exam. The answer may have been copied verbatim from a textbook to the crib notes and from the notes to the exam.

Possible copying can be detected by keeping track of where students sit and examining the responses of adjacent students for answers that are suspiciously similar. Student seating can be tracked by assigning students to seats for exams, numbering answer sheets and booklets and distributing them in numerical order, or having students leave their exams on their seats and collecting them in seating order. One must use this technique judiciously because, as Box 4.4 shows, there can be innocent explanations for similar answers.

For multiple-choice tests, it is possible to calculate the probability of the extent to which two students' patterns of answers are similar due to chance factors alone. A low probability of similarity could mean that one student

BOX 4.4
Limitations of Error Similarity Analysis

- The statistical procedures assume that no two questions on the exam deal with the same concept—an assumption that is probably not viable for most exams.
- Accurate computation of the necessary statistics requires a test that is long or difficult enough so that the average number of errors per student is 15 when there are five response options from which to choose.
- Because the analyses contrast patterns of errors made by adjacent students with patterns of errors made by nonadjacent students, one must keep track of where each student sat during the exam.
- The fact that most of these procedures focus on errors is problematic: Poor students will make more errors than good students even when they are not cheating, and a higher number of errors increases the likelihood that one poor student's error pattern will be similar to another poor student's error pattern. Thus, error similarity analyses "are inherently biased against students who perform poorly and [are] less likely to detect the 'smart' cheater" (Dwyer & Hecht, 1996, p. 129).
- There are a number of innocent explanations for similar errors, such as:

  - Two students study together and, in the process, share their misconceptions about the material covered by the test.
  - Poorly worded questions and ambiguous response options lead students to innocently choose similar wrong answers.
  - If an error exists on the scoring key, students who choose the correct answer appear to have chosen the same "incorrect" response.

- Just because the probability of two students having the same pattern of errors is very low does not necessarily mean that one copied from the other. Although the low probability value indicates that innocent similarity is unlikely, it is a statistical truism that even highly improbable events do sometimes occur, albeit extremely rarely. As Dwyer and Hecht (1996) noted, "even though the probability of being struck by lightning is very small, many people are struck by lightning every year" (p. 128).
- The use of the results of error similarity analyses as evidence of cheating in disciplinary hearings may be open to legal challenge. The law requires college and university disciplinary board hearings to adhere to the principles of due process and equal protection (e.g., Gehring & Pavela, 1994). Error similarity analyses might fail the due process test because there are reasonable alternatives to cheating as explanations for similar response patterns. Error similarity analyses might also fail the equal protection test because, as noted earlier, they are biased against low-ability students. Therefore, similarity may not be sufficient evidence of cheating from a legal point of view, but must be supported by other evidence.

Note. Based on Bellezza and Bellezza (1989) and Dwyer and Hecht (1996).

copied from the other; that is, the likelihood that they independently choose the same responses is very low. Because the focus of these analyses is usually on patterns of errors, and students who know the material should have similar patterns of correct responses, this technique is often referred to as *error similarity analysis*.

There are a number of mathematical procedures for conducting error similarity analyses, most of which have been converted to computer programs (see review by Frary, 1992). However, because these procedures have a number of severe limitations (see Box 4.4), we do not recommend their use: It is probably more efficient to take steps to prevent cheating than it is to try to detect it and deal with after the fact. If these methods are used, they should probably be used only as a means to identify potential cheaters, whose behavior can then be monitored more closely in the future to prevent cheating or detect it with greater certainty.

Table 4.3 summarizes our suggestions for preventing and detecting cheating on examinations. Many of these suggestions are labor-intensive, but research has shown them to be effective.

THE ROLE OF STUDENTS IN MAINTAINING ACADEMIC HONESTY

Thus far, we have focused on what instructors can do to prevent and detect academic dishonesty. In this section, we comment on the role students play in these processes.

Prevention

In his review of the research literature on cheating, Whitley (1998) found that one of the strongest correlates of students' willingness to engage in academic dishonesty was their perception of the normative climate: Students who believed that their peers disapproved of academic dishonesty were less likely to cheat than those who perceived a normative climate that was indifferent to or supportive of dishonesty. In addition, the lower rates of cheating found at colleges and universities with honor codes were due in part to normative climates at those institutions that support academic integrity and condemn dishonesty (McCabe & Trevino, 1993; McCabe et al., 1999). Therefore, students have the capacity to help prevent academic dishonesty by expressing disapproval of it.

TABLE 4.3
Techniques for Preventing and Detecting Academic
Dishonesty: Examinations

Form of Dishonesty	Prevention	Detection
General	Carefully proctor exams	Carefully observe test takers preferably from the back of the room so they can't see the proctor without turning around
Stealing exams prior to administration	Establish stringent test security procedures Do not allow student employees to copy exams Store exams on computer diskettes, not on hard drives; keep diskettes locked up Shred copies spoiled during duplication	Number all exam copies immediately, and periodically check for missing copies
Using crib notes	Allow the use of notes Be explicit about what materials students may and may not use during exams Require students to leave books, coats, and so on at the back of the room Require students who wear baseball caps to turn the brim to the rear Provide all paper, exam booklets, and so on to the students at the start of the exam; if students bring their own exam booklets, collect them, stamp them with a code, and redistribute them randomly Attach blank pages to the test when scratch paper is needed	Be alert for answers that look *too good*

TABLE 4.3 (continued)

Form of Dishonesty	Prevention	Detection
	Require students to turn in exam if they must leave the room Ban unnecessary electronic devices from the exam	
Copying from other test takers; exchanging information with other test takers	Spread students out, increasing the space between rows if possible Randomly assign students to different seats for each exam (students prefer to copy from friends with whom they've made arrangements) Use alternate exam forms with questions in different orders, and response options in different orders in multiple-choice items Use alternate exam forms with different questions of equal difficulty or grade within test form Distribute alternate forms in a checkerboard pattern so each student is surrounded by a form different than his or hers Use essay or short answer rather than multiple-choice questions Require students to keep their answers covered Do not allow students to share pencils, erasers, and so on once the exam has started, or require students to use pencils supplied by the instructor	Watch for similarities in patterns of errors Have students leave exams on their seats; compare neighbors' responses

TABLE 4.3 (continued)

Form of Dishonesty	Prevention	Detection
	Require students to move if collaboration is suspected Ban unnecessary electronic devices from the exam	
Having the test taken by a substitute (ringer)	Check student identification at entry	Check student identification when the test is turned in
Getting information from test takers in earlier exam sessions or when taking a makeup exam	Use different questions in different exam sessions	
Changing answers during posttest reviews	Tell students that answer sheets are copied before the review Mark correct answer in ink on answer sheet X-out space left blank at the end of essay or short answer responses Annotate questions not answered on answer sheet or booklet	Copy answer sheets prior to the review
Getting information from test files	Number all copies of exams and ensure that all are returned; number answer sheets to know who had which exam copy Shred old exams before throwing them out Change test questions frequently	

Note. Adapted from A. C. Singhal & P. Johnson, "How to Halt Student Dishonesty, *College Student Journal,* 1983, *17,* pp. 13–19. Adapted with permission of *College Student Journal,* P.O. Box 8508, Spring Hill Station, Mobile, AL 36689–9508.

However, although most students condemn academic dishonesty when responding to surveys, they appear reluctant to express their disapproval in other ways (Hendershott et al., 1999; Jendrek, 1992). For example, Jendrek found that 61% of the sample of students she surveyed reported having personally observed some form of cheating, but that 55% said they ignored it. Although an additional 39% said that they discussed the incident with students other than the cheater, only 5% said they told the cheater that they disapproved of the behavior.

Therefore, students' disapproval of academic dishonesty is only sometimes communicated to other students. One role played by the in-class discussions of academic integrity that we recommended in chapter 3 is that of providing a forum for students to express their disapproval of academic dishonesty; such discussions help develop a normative climate that supports academic integrity. When, at the beginning of the term, we have asked the kinds of questions listed at the beginning of this chapter (such as, "Have you ever observed other students cheating and how did you feel about that?"), spontaneous comments from the student audience have included:

> "It makes me sick to see other students cheat. I feel like I am part of it somehow. It makes it hard for me to concentrate on my own work, and I resent that."
> "I study hard to get a good education, and I want the grades I have earned. When I see a student just copying off another student or one of my friends brags about copying a term paper off the Web, I feel like exploding."
> "I don't respect students who cheat. I know a bunch of students who I would never hire if I was an employer."

No student, in our experience, has ever spoken up in favor of cheating probably because such public remarks would be socially undesirable and academically risky. However, should a pro-cheating remark ever be elicited, it would provide an opportunity to point out tactfully the wrongmindedness of such thinking.

Detection

Students are clearly in a position to detect the academic dishonesty of other students, as evidenced by Jendrek's (1992) finding that 61% of her sample reported having witnessed other students cheating. However, students are very reluctant to report their peers' academic dishonesty. Jendrek, for example, found that only 1% of the students in her sample who had witnessed cheating reported it as required by their university. Some did not report the cheating because they did not care about it: 36% reported that their emotional response to the cheating incident was one of indifference. However, 56% reported feeling anger or disgust, but nonetheless made no report. Why not? Box 4.5 lists some of the factors that emerged from a survey conducted by McCabe et al. (1999). These findings and others (e.g., Jendrek, 1992) indicate that suggestions for facilitating student reporting of academic dishonesty, such as anonymous hot lines (e.g., Singhal & Johnson, 1983), would probably not be effective. Indeed, when Hollinger and Lanza-Kaduce (1996) asked students for their views on such a hot line, only 16% thought it would help to deter academic dishonesty.

The results of the Jendrek (1992) and McCabe et al. (1999) studies suggest that reporting academic dishonesty, or even expressing their disapproval to dishonest students, requires students to develop a sense of personal responsibility for the academic integrity of their colleges and universities. The effects of an integrity-supportive normative climate on student reporting are illustrated by McCabe's finding (reported in Cole & McCabe, 1996) that 56% of students at colleges and universities with honor codes said they would be likely or very likely to report another student for cheating compared with 17% of students at other institutions. For many colleges and universities, developing and maintaining such a sense of responsibility will require major changes in their cultures and normative climates. We discuss such changes in the chapter 6.

Despite students' reluctance to snitch on their peers, we suggest using class discussions of academic dishonesty to encourage students to report any instances that they witness. The benefits of doing so are twofold: Some students might actually do it, and some students contemplating cheating might be dissuaded by fear of being reported.

THE CHALLENGE OF DISTANCE EDUCATION

As distance education becomes more common, the question arises of how instructors can prevent and detect cheating at remote sites (Randall, 1998). Although the problem might seem almost insurmountable, Randall pointed out that many of the techniques used in the regular classroom can

BOX 4.5
Reasons Students Give for Not Reporting Cheaters

- Fear of being responsible for negative effects on cheaters, especially the severe consequences, such as suspension or expulsion, that may be policy at honor code schools.
- Fear of making an enemy.
- Conflicting demands of loyalty posed by friendship if the cheater is a friend.
- Fear of making an unfounded accusation—that the student might actually be innocent.
- Belief that "squealing" is a worse offense than cheating.
- Peer pressure against "squealing."
- Belief that instructors or administrators may not be willing or able to take action against cheaters.
- An individualistic campus culture that encourages people to ignore anything that does not affect them directly.

Source. McCabe et al. (1999).

be applied to the distance education classroom especially if a proctor is present for each class session. These techniques include discussions of academic integrity, use of proctors during in-class writing assignments to prevent plagiarism and unauthorized collaboration, and use of multiple exam forms, spaced seating, and close proctoring during exams. Instructors can also point out to students that the distance education environment places special trust in students' integrity because the instructor is not personally present to monitor their behavior. Box 4.6 lists some additional control measures that can be used.

We also recommend that distance education instructors establish personal contact with site proctors. Use initial contacts to establish collaborative relationships with the proctors, explaining their role in the educational process and discussing the problem of academic dishonesty and ways to prevent and control it. Use later contacts to ask the proctors about the classroom climates at their sites; students may be more willing to voice complaints and discuss their academic problems with the proctor whom they see on a regular basis than with the literally distant instructor. Use the information gained to modify the course content to better meet students' needs.

BOX 4.6
Tactics for Controlling Cheating in Distanced Education Classes

- Form relationships with students using chat rooms and discussion postings.
- Call students to discuss points covered in exams, papers, and homework assignments.
- Ask students how they obtained the information they used in papers; students who plagiarize may not be able to describe the research process.
- If students take exams at home, have them install web cameras so the instructor can monitor them during exams.
- Have students provide writing samples during the first class period and e-mail them immediately to provide a baseline to which terms papers can be compared. Chat room and discussion board postings can also be used for this purpose.

Source. Carnevale (1999).

SUMMARY

The focus of this chapter was on preventing and detecting academic dishonesty in the classroom. We began by outlining a few techniques that are generally applicable to the problem: discussing academic dishonesty with students, identifying students at risk for academic dishonesty, and increasing the risk of having dishonest behaviors detected. We then made some specific suggestions for preventing and detecting dishonesty in homework assignments, lab reports, term papers, and examinations.

In this chapter and chapter 3 we have made a rather large (and, perhaps, overwhelming) number of suggestions and recommendations about preventing and detecting academic dishonesty. Many of these techniques are time-consuming and labor-intensive in other ways, but many of them provide benefits in addition to discouraging academic dishonesty. For example, requiring students to write multiple drafts of papers and make oral reports on their topics enhances students' written and oral presentation skills and probably also enhances learning. In addition, honest students will appreciate instructors' attempts to prevent cheating and plagiarism. In summary, these are what we see as the most important points:

- Develop a classroom climate that fosters academic integrity by treating students fairly and being available to students to confer about class-related matters.

- Teach students the skills they need to avoid problems such as plagiarism. If these skills should have been developed in a prerequisite course, discuss the need to cover these topics with your department's curriculum committee.

- Make it clear to students that you value academic integrity by including a statement on academic integrity in your syllabi and discussing integrity with your classes.

- Review your institution's policies on academic integrity with your classes.

- For gray areas, such as collaboration, be explicit about what you do and do not permit.

- Clearly state the consequences for any violations of academic integrity. *Always follow to the letter your institution's policies in this regard.*

- Carefully monitor exams and use as many other control techniques (such as multiple forms of exams) as possible. In large classes, use additional proctors if they are available.

- Use as many techniques as are feasible to prevent and discourage plagiarism.

- Commit yourself to fully investigate and follow through on every case of suspected dishonesty. *For your legal protection, always follow to the letter your institution's policies in this regard.*

5

Confronting and Dealing With Academic Dishonesty

◆ ◆ ◆

This chapter discusses the unpleasant process of confronting and dealing with instances of academic dishonesty. We offer suggestions for handling academic dishonesty when it is first detected (e.g., while proctoring an exam), discuss the issues involved in resolving cases of suspected and actual dishonesty, and comment on appropriate sanctions and punishments for academic dishonesty.

WHAT ABOUT JUST DOING NOTHING?

Because confronting students suspected of student dishonesty is among the most onerous features of the teaching profession (Keith-Spiegel et al., 1998), it may be extremely tempting to justify inaction when suspicions are aroused. Besides viewing cheating as "a positive form of collaborative learning" (as presented in chapt. 1), Box 5.1 provides examples of other possible rationalizations for turning one's eyes away.

It is true that some administrators may be so unsupportive that they cause faculty members to think twice before getting involved in a doubly noxious situation: They must deal with not only a student they suspect of cheating, but also with an indifferent or obstructive administrator. It is also true that some students will reap unfortunate consequences for unethical actions in the future. Of course, dealing with cheating does take some time and mustering of courage. Furthermore, we know that all human beings have frailties. However, as noted in chapter 1, ignoring academic incidents altogether contributes to larger problems for students, our institutions, society, and even for ourselves. Dealing with cheating in a devious manner, such as is illustrated in Box 5.2, does not solve the dilemma either.

BOX 5.1
Rationalizations for Instructor Inaction

"The administration will not support me."

"It will all catch up with them sooner or later."

"I put in enough time on this job as it is and I am still behind. I don't have time to deal with this."

"Everyone makes mistakes."

"I did it a couple of times when I was in college and didn't get caught. I turned out all right."

"I don't know for absolutely 100% sure that he cheated."

"I was trained as an educator, not an investigator."

"Dealing with this will cause more problems than it is worth."

"I will end up getting sued or retaliated against in some way. It's a lose-lose situation."

"She's got so many problems as it is. She doesn't need what I would have to do with her."

"I don't want to be the one to blemish the academic career of a young person."

Many instructors do nothing when they believe that they do not have, or cannot collect, enough evidence to make a solid case (Keith-Spiegel et al., 1998). Although we should not go about accusing students on flimsy grounds, we often must process cases on evidence that is not air tight. However, a less-than-sure case should not be ignored as a way to avoid the responsibility to maintain integrity in our classrooms. Even if the result of a confrontation is inconclusive, the process of inquiry can still be ended in a satisfactory manner, and the experience could even have a salutary effect if the student was actually guilty. Similarly, an instructor's concluding that no wrong-doing occurred can have a positive effect on the teacher-student relationship if handled tactfully. See Box 5.3 for two examples.

DISCLAIMERS

Three disclaimers are required before we begin our discussion of how to confront and manage academic dishonesty. First, we make a number of suggestions for handling cases of detected or suspected dishonesty, not all of

BOX 5.2
An Unethical Method for Resolving Incidents of Suspected Unethical Behavior

We have heard of a way of dealing with instances of academic dishonesty that we do not recommend. Proponents of this method allegedly believe that they have found a method of punishing cheaters without having to go through either a formal or informal resolution procedure. Indeed, even the student does not know that he or she has been judged and punished!

Here is how it works. The instructor, convinced that a student has cheated, simply figures out how to give the student a lower grade. For example, any subjective assignment or activity is graded lower than it would have been otherwise. Or a pop quiz is given on a day that the targeted student is absent. Or if the student requested a letter of recommendation, the instructor provides a negative one.

Although such a resolution technique may seem, at first blush, a clever way for instructors to "make things even" without enduring discomfort, it fails miserably on several grounds. First, it is cowardly. Second, it does not afford innocent students any opportunity to defend themselves. Third, guilty students learn nothing about the consequences of their behaviors. Finally, the evidence on which the judgment was made could be in error or misunderstood, causing innocent students to be wrongfully condemned.

---

which may be consistent with the policies in effect at your college or university. *In all cases of differences between our advice and your institution's policies, you must follow your institution's policies.* Failure to follow institutional policy is not only a violation of your contract with the institution, but could also lead to legal difficulties (Gehring & Pavela, 1994; Kibler et al., 1988). If you think that your institution's policies could be improved, we encourage you to work to change them, but never ignore them. Second, although we discuss some legal issues, we are not attorneys, so our comments should not be construed as legal advice. *If you decide that you require legal advice in handling a case of academic dishonesty, consult the attorney retained by your college or university.* Finally, our suggestions cannot cover all possible contingencies; they should be modified as necessary to fit specific situations.

BOX 5.3
Two Inconclusive Confrontations

THE SALUTARY EFFECT

Although one of our colleagues was convinced that Susie repeatedly looked directly at her neighbor's exam paper, it would be his word against hers should the matter ever be adjudicated. Our colleague called Susie into the office and described the behavior that concerned him. Susie adamantly denied any inference that she was cheating. She claimed that she always moved her head around when she was nervous. Our friend ended the session by commenting that such behavior appeared to be suspicious, but that he would not pursue the matter further. He also informed her that he expected that she would control her head-moving behavior during future exams.

On the next exam, Susie kept her eyes on her own paper. The few times she looked up, she found herself in a locked glance with our colleague who focused in on her during most of the hour. He believed that Susie's experience with a close call, followed by receiving special attention, might have sent the message home that cheating is risky and not a matter that instructors take lightly.

THE APOLOGY

An instructor was suspicious when she received two written assignments that were very similar in structure and selected references. Although the narrow topic that was assigned could have resulted in coincidental similarities, she called in both students (separately) to her office and informed them of her concerns. Each student denied having anything to do with the other's paper. Both denied even knowing each other beyond casual encounters in her classroom. Both were able to produce copies of the articles with their own notes in the margins and early outlines.

The instructor considered the materials and concluded that her initial judgment was in error. She called the students in again and apologized for causing them distress. She explained that her obligation to investigate came from her strong commitment to integrity and the welfare of her students. Both students accepted her apology, adding that they understood what she did and why she did it. She reported no negative after effects.

SUSPECTED DISHONESTY

When you suspect one of your students of cheating on an exam or of turning in a plagiarized term paper or homework assignment, an awful feeling in the pit of the stomach is a common first response. But what actions should you take? Box 5.4 offers some suggestions.

BOX 5.4
Coping With Stress

Dealing with cases of suspected or actual academic dishonesty is one of the most stressful aspects of being a college or university instructor. Therefore, we provide a few suggestions for dealing with that stress:

• Seek out a trusted colleague known for sensitivity to ethical matters and discuss the incident. However, do not identify the student unless the colleague needs to know the student's identity because of an administrative position he or she holds, such as department chair. Naming a suspected student to anyone who does not have an official need to know may make you vulnerable to legal action (Gehring, 1998).

• Keep in mind that cheating is, unfortunately, common and therefore does not reflect on you personally; you are not in a unique situation. Stress is sometimes lessened when people realize they are not alone with a dilemma.

• Remind yourself that most students cheat because of self-interest, not as a way or hurting their instructors. Most are completely unaware of the impact that uncovering an act of academic dishonesty has on their teachers.

• Consider all of your options for dealing with the situation and their possible outcomes, make a plan, and stick to it. Stress is usually alleviated by establishing a course of action.

• Resist easy outs, such as ignoring the evidence. Ignoring the situation might only lead to regrets later.

• Think about why it is important to quash academic dishonesty. Stress is often lowered when one is committed, even when making the commitment and following through on it is anxiety-arousing.

• Involve yourself in enjoyable, diverting activities rather than letting the matter dominate your thinking.

Exams

If your suspicions are aroused during an exam, the first thing to do, if another proctor is present, is to ask that proctor to observe the suspected student's behavior. Try to make that request discretely so that the student is not tipped off. The proctor's observations may indicate that you were mistaken, in which case no further action is necessary. If the proctor agrees with your conclusion about the student's behavior, the proctor becomes an additional witness to the offense.

At this point, regardless of whether a proctor is present, it is often useful to stand where the cheating student can see you and stare at him or her with a concentrated look of disapproval. The student's awareness that you are watching will frequently stop the behavior, and you can confront the student after the exam without disrupting surrounding students.

If the look does not stop the student's behavior, we suggest that you take the following steps *if* you can do so without unduly disturbing the exam takers near the offending student; otherwise wait until the student completes the exam before confronting him or her.

- Inform the student that you think he or she has been copying or using crib notes, as the case may be. You should try to do this while minimally disturbing the other students.

- If you suspect the student of copying, require the student to move to another seat—one separated from other students if possible.

- If you suspect the student of using crib notes, confiscate the notes if possible, but do not use physical force to do so. *Regardless of whether you are able to confiscate the notes, allow the student to complete the exam, telling the student that you will contact him or her later to resolve the issue.*

- If the student objects to your requests, remind the student that he or she can use the time remaining in the testing period to step into a quiet corner of the room to discuss the matter without disturbing the other students or to complete the test.

- Record the names of the students (if known, or can be easily ascertained from a seating chart) sitting next to the suspected student. These students may be witnesses to the cheating. If you later ask these students if they saw anything that might indicate that someone was cheating, phrase your questions carefully to avoid accusing a specific individual and to avoid biasing their answers. Alternatively, you could send their names as potential witnesses to the academic integrity hearing board if the matter is to be resolved through a formal hearing process.

- Make a note of the problematic test questions. If copying is suspected, you can compare the answers of these students to those of the suspected student.

Term Papers and Homework Assignments

If you suspect that a student has copied a homework assignment from another student or has plagiarized part of a term paper, the first step is to consider the likelihood that the problem was caused by misunderstanding, ignorance, or negligence rather than intentional dishonesty. For example, did you clearly state the limits of collaboration on homework assignments or take-home exams? If there is any ambiguity, it might be best to resolve the question in the student's favor and revise your instructions the next time the assignment is given. If a brief passage appears to have been plagiarized, is it a case of intentional dishonesty or did the student not understand how to properly cite a source? Could the student have carelessly omitted the proper citation? If the student does not know proper citation procedures, additional instruction is probably in order; if the student was careless, lowering the student's grade on the paper accompanied by a marginal note on the need for careful citation is probably the most appropriate action.

If innocent explanations are unlikely, keep the original of the suspect paper or assignment and return a copy to the student. This procedure prevents the student from making any alterations to the work before the issue is resolved. You should follow the same procedure if you suspect copying on an exam based on similarity of answers. However, bear in mind the possibility of innocent explanations for similar work, such as students' sharing misconceptions while studying together.

Student Reports of Other Students Cheating

Occasionally, a student will come to an instructor and report having observed someone else cheating or that another student plagiarized a paper or engaged in another form of academic dishonesty. These situations can be delicate because, in many cases, students will be violating student norms by snitching on another student and might feel nervous about doing so. The first thing to do, then, is to reassure the student by thanking him or her for coming and letting you know about the situation. (Because of its connotations, it is probably best not to use the word *inform*.)

If you are already aware of the incident, tell the student so and that you are taking action on it. If the student asks what action you are taking, reply (truthfully) that all student academic information is confidential, so you cannot discuss the matter with anyone who is not directly involved. You should also ask the student whether he or she would be willing to be a witness at a judicial board hearing if one were to be held.

If the allegation is new to you, get as much information about the incident as the student can (or is willing) to provide. Frequently, students are unwilling to name the culprit, so you must ask. If the reporting student refuses to provide a name, do not pressure the student: Pressure is unlikely to result in the information you want and will only make the student reluctant to talk to you in the future about any topic. Instead, point out to the student that there is little you can do without knowing who the offender is. If this reminder does not elicit the offender's name, tell the student that all you can do is watch everyone's work more closely in the future and that you will do so. Finally, be sure to thank the student for coming to you.

If the reporting student does provide the offender's name, ask the student whether he or she would be willing to be a witness at a judicial board hearing if one were to be held. Often students will say "no"—that they do not want to get involved publicly. As with the student who does not want to provide a name, remind the reluctant witness that your options are limited if he or she is not willing to testify. If your institution does not allow instructors to handle cases of suspected dishonesty on their own and requires a formal hearing in all cases, inform the student that there is nothing you can do without the witness' testimony. If the student still refuses, tell him or her that you will do what you can and thank the student for coming to you.

One action that you can take, even if the reporting student does not give you the offender's name, is to tell the entire class that it has come to your attention that there was a problem with cheating on the last test (or whatever the offense was). Let the class members know that you are disappointed with the news because your trust in them may have been unjustified. Invite any students who have information to share, or who want to discuss the situation, to visit you in your office. Also inform them that because of this situation you will be monitoring everyone's work more closely in the future.

Given that most students are reluctant to report their peers (Jendrek, 1992; McCabe et al., 1999), should faculty members encourage students to directly confront those students whom they observe cheating? This question has been debated in informal discussions, but no consensus has been reached. Those who favor encouraging student-to-student confrontation do so on the grounds that disapproval by one's peers may be an effective deterrent in the future. However, others worry that students who confront their peers may put themselves in harm's way (e.g., being rejected or retaliated against). Further, it is not the responsibility of individual students to deal with cheating peers by themselves. In our opinion, it is better not to openly encourage students to confront cheaters: The potential consequences outweigh the potential benefits. In addition, peer disapproval of cheaters can be elicited in more controlled ways, such as in class discussions (see chapt. 3).

RESOLVING CASES OF DISHONESTY

Faculty members can take two courses of action in resolving a case of suspected academic dishonesty (Risacher & Slonaker, 1996). The first is what we call *informal resolution*. Here the faculty member deals directly with the student without involving institutional administrators, judicial boards, or other disciplinary bodies of the college or university in the resolution process. The second course of action is what we call *formal resolution*, which involves administrators or disciplinary bodies.

Important Note

Some colleges and universities do not allow informal resolution of cases of suspected academic dishonesty. Other institutions may allow informal resolution under some circumstances but not others, or they may require the instructor to submit reports of informal resolutions. As we noted earlier, *you must scrupulously follow the procedures laid down by your institution for resolving cases of suspected academic dishonesty. If those procedures do not permit informal resolution, do not use it; use the formal procedures established by your college or university.* The case reported in Box 5.5 illustrates the consequences of ignoring policy.

Informal Resolution

Most faculty members seem to prefer informal resolution to formal resolution. Jendrek (1989) and Singhal (1982) found that only 20% of their respondents who had dealt with cases of academic dishonesty used formal procedures. However, this preference for informal resolution predominates at institutions without honor codes. McCabe (1993) asked 789 faculty members from 16 college and universities what they would do if faced with a case of academic dishonesty. He found that only 33% of the faculty at institutions without honor codes said they would use formal resolution, compared with 68% of faculty members at institutions with honor codes. Although McCabe's data do not address the question of why this difference exists, it is likely that many honor code institutions do not allow informal resolution because their policies require the involvement of student body representatives in the resolution process (e.g., McCabe & Trevino, 1993).

Advantages of Informal Resolution. Faculty preference for informal resolution is not surprising; it has several advantages from the faculty member's viewpoint:

BOX 5.5
The Consequences of Ignoring Policy

A professor was standing unobserved near a bench outside the classroom watching one student furiously write while looking back and forth between her notebook and that of her friend. It seemed abundantly clear to the professor that one student was simply copying the problem set answers from the paper of a willing accomplice. After a few minutes, the perturbed professor approached the two students and informed them that they would both get a grade of zero on the assignment.

The students contacted the university ombudsperson, complaining that they had been wrongfully punished and denied due process. They testified that one was only checking answers, not copying them. The professor was surprised to be called by the Associate Provost, informing him that he had violated the school's policy for handling and sanctioning acts of academic dishonesty. In the end, it was the professor who underwent an inquiry, and the charges against the students were dropped on the grounds that the matter was handled improperly.

• It allows simple resolution of cases in which the problem was caused by misconception, ignorance, or negligence.

• Although formal procedures can determine that an apparent act of dishonesty was, in fact, caused by innocent factors, informal procedures allow for immediate corrective action with less anxiety for the student and without the stigma of being accused of dishonesty.

• If the student admits to dishonesty, informal resolution allows faculty members to exercise their traditional roles of instructor and mentor, both in terms of the ethical issues involved and the academic exercise involved: The student's learning can be fostered by having him or her redo the assignment.

• If given the option, most students prefer informal resolution. This way the matter stays between the student and the faculty member, and the teacher–student relationship is likely to suffer less disruption than would occur in the wake of a formal hearing.

• It is less time-consuming (and probably less stressful in most cases) than formal resolution.

Disadvantages of Informal Resolution. Despite the attractive elements inherent in resolving academic dishonesty cases informally, there are a number of disadvantages.

• The instructor is personally affected by the cheating incident, which may impair his or her ability to deal with the matter objectively.

- Most college instructors have no special expertise in conflict resolution, which may hamper their ability to manage the situation effectively.

- Most college instructors have no expertise in the potential legal issues that could arise when dealing with instances of academic dishonesty. As such, they may jeopardize the student's rights and, in doing so, create complications for themselves.

- College instructors probably differ in their judgments of the seriousness of certain acts and the penalties they are willing to impose. In the absence of access to a larger picture, sanctions for the same act may vary markedly from instructor to instructor creating confusion and later accusations of unfairness.

- Acting alone, without the active involvement of the larger organization, the instructor can feel insecure and vulnerable. Some instructors, especially those from institutions that require an attempt at an informal resolution before involving the next level, may therefore prefer to avoid the issue altogether.

- Unless institutional policy is very clear with regard to the informal resolution process (and most are not), the instructor's resolution of the case may be questioned later.

- Unless institutional policy requires that records of informal resolutions be kept in a central archive, repeat offenders may go undetected.

Recommended Procedure. How should informal resolution be carried out? First, if you are not already knowledgeable about your institution's policies, thoroughly review and adhere to them. Seek advice if anything is unclear. To the extent that your institutional policy allows, we recommend that you ask the student for a meeting, informing him or her of exactly what you perceive the problem to be. You should also inform the student that the meeting is not mandatory, but that if the student refuses to meet the matter will be referred for formal resolution. Also inform the student that he or she can request formal resolution instead of meeting with you. We recommend that you include the department chair (or a faculty member designated by the chair) in the meeting as a witness. If so, you should also inform the student of that and perhaps allow the student to be accompanied by a faculty member of his or her choice. Ideally, you should inform the student in writing, or follow up on a conversation with a memorandum to the student, to prevent any misunderstanding. See Box 5.6 for an example; if you use it, be sure to modify it to conform with your institution's policies and procedures.

When discussing the issue with the student, present it as one of resolving apparent irregularities in the student's work rather than as an accusation of dishonesty. Accusations are likely to lead to hostility, defensiveness, and refusal to discuss the issue, whereas an atmosphere of inquiry is more likely to result in cooperation. Therefore, you should explain the problem you

BOX 5.6
Sample Memo to Student Confirming a Meeting Concerning Suspected Academic Dishonesty

Dear _____,

As I mentioned in our conversation earlier today, there appears to be an irregularity in your library homework assignment for PSY 284: You and _____ turned in papers in which all 10 questions had identical incorrect answers. At first glance, this situation appears to be an instance of you and _____ sharing answers despite the fact that the instructions on the homework assignment sheet specified that students were to work independently.

During our conversation today, we agreed to meet in my office on Monday, February 28th, at 10:00 a.m. to discuss this matter. As I said this morning, you are not required to meet with me, but if you decide not to meet, I will refer this matter to the Dean because it appears to be a violation of the College's academic integrity policy (see pp. ___ to ___ of the Student Handbook). If you would prefer to have a third party resolve this matter rather than discuss it with me, you can refer the matter to the Dean yourself, following the procedures in the Student Handbook.

If you change your mind about meeting with me on Monday, please let me know. Otherwise, I will see you then.

Sincerely,

found in the student's work (e.g., part of a paper appears to be taken verbatim from a source) and ask the student to explain how this came to be. If the student asks a question along the lines of "If I did copy it, what will happen to me?", fully explain the consequences.

If the student provides an explanation that rules out dishonesty, tell the student that, now that he or she has explained the situation, it is clear that (depending on the situation) no problem exists or that the only problem appears to be that the student has made an error. For example, the student might not know how to properly cite sources. You should then move on to correct the source of the student's error. At the end of the meeting, thank the student for coming in to resolve the matter.

If the student admits to dishonesty (or agrees to a resolution that does not include an admission of dishonesty), you should have the student agree to the penalty you choose to impose. Ideally, this agreement should be in writing. The document need not cite dishonesty as the reason for the penalty; it could simply say something along the lines of, "I agree that zero is the most appropriate grade for my work on [name of assignment]" or "I agree that I should not receive credit for the questions numbered _____ on test number _____." Give the student a copy of the document and keep one for your records. Try to close the meeting on an optimistic note, but tell the student that, because of the problem just resolved, his or her future work will receive special scrutiny.

If you find the student's explanation to be insufficient, if the student refuses to give an explanation, or if the students admits dishonesty but refuses to accept the penalty, you have two options. One is to drop the matter, which you may have to do if you believe that you do not have adequate evidence to initiate formal resolution. The second option is, of course, formal resolution. Whichever course of action you choose, inform the student. However, if you do not initiate formal procedures, also tell the student, that because it appears that a problem has arisen, you will monitor all students' work more closely in the future. In addition, inform the class that you suspect cheating has been going on and you will be watching things more closely.

Penalties. When determining the appropriate penalty to administer in an informal resolution, you should first consult your institution's policy on handling cases of academic dishonesty: The policy may prescribe certain penalties or limit the kinds of penalties that instructors may administer as part of an informal resolution. *Be sure to adhere strictly to any prescribed punishments or limitations on punishments set by the policy.* Although some institutions may allow an instructor to assign a grade of "F" in the course as a result of an informal resolution, we do not recommend that you do this even if it is permitted. We believe that the decision to assign such a severe penalty should be made by disinterested parties. Therefore, if you believe that failure in the course is appropriate, we recommend that you refer the case for formal resolution.

Formal Resolution

Formal resolution of suspected academic dishonesty can be initiated in several ways:

- Faculty members can immediately initiate it when they suspect academic dishonesty has occurred.

- Faculty members may decide on formal resolution in situations in which informal resolution fails.
- The student may request formal resolution in lieu of informal resolution.
- The student may use formal channels to appeal the outcome of an informal resolution.

Because formal resolution of academic dishonesty cases is primarily an institutional function, we defer most of our discussion of it until the next chapter, which focuses on institutional responses to academic dishonesty. In this chapter, we simply note some of the major advantages that formal resolution has over informal resolution to help instructors make a choice between the two processes.

- Formal resolution places a buffer between the instructor and the student (and sometimes the student's parents). Such a buffer can be useful when feelings run high, protecting the faculty member from the student's anger and, as sometimes happens, the student from the faculty member's anger.
- Formal resolution procedures are designed to protect the student's legal rights and therefore help to shield the instructor and institution from allegations of violation of those rights.
- Because records of formal resolutions are maintained at a central location, the process can detect and appropriately punish repeat offenders. Unless institutional policy requires that informal resolutions be reported to a central office, career cheaters can keep on offending as long as they never get caught more than once in the same instructor's courses—or if they do get caught, the instructor handles the matter informally.
- Because it is a formal disciplinary process, more severe punishments can be imposed if the student is found guilty.

Because formal procedures require more paperwork and procedural decorum, they are also likely to be experienced with a sense of dread. Box 5.7 and Box 5.8 offer some suggestions for approaching and participating in a formal hearing.

ON BEING A STUDENT ADVISOR

Some school policies allow students accused of academic dishonesty to select a faculty member to help them prepare their materials and/or attend the formal hearing with them. If you accept a request to serve in this role, we suggest the following:

BOX 5.7
Preparing Yourself for a Formal Hearing

Faculty with whom we have spoken have compared the role of presenting a case against a student in a formal hearing to being on trial oneself. To protect due process rights of students, formal hearings are, by necessity, structured—sometimes to the point of appearing ceremonious. The faculty member may not be allowed to have counsel or a faculty supporter present, whereas the accused student can be allowed a number of supporters, including parents and legal counsel.

Some steps should be taken, however, to assist you in gaining confidence and reducing stress. (See other hints regarding stress reduction in Box 5.4.)

• Be familiar with all rules, procedures, or policies under which the panel operates. If anything is not clear to you, seek clarification well in advance of the hearing.

• Do not speak to the involved student about the matter. If the student or one of the student's agents instigates a contact, refer the person to the office in your institution that has oversight of academic integrity matters. Recognize that the matter is no longer subject to informal resolution. Any contact initiated by you may be viewed as coercion or harassment and reported as such during the hearing.

• Know exactly with whom you will be dealing. Who are the players and what are their roles?

• Find out if you are allowed to bring someone into the hearing with you and, if so, what functions he or she can serve. Be sure that both you and the other person fully understand what roles he or she can and cannot play in the hearing. For example, is the other person allowed to speak for you?

• Compile and organize your records, testimony, and the relevant chronology of events. The hearing is no time to be shuffling through papers only to find that you do not have what you were looking for with you.

• Do not do anything impulsive regardless of how emotionally upset you might become. We know of a case where a beleaguered professor, outraged by having to undergo a formal hearing involving two students whose defense was that they were set up by a racist teacher, wrote a scathing letter about "the misuse of 'the race card' " that was published in the school paper. The response to its inflammatory style was very hurtful to the professor in the long run.

• Although you may find aspects of the system at your institution inadequate or faulty, we suggest that you withhold criticism until after the formal hearing process is completed. (We do encourage later follow through with remediation activities; see chapt. 6.)

• Be patient. Depending on your school policy, you may have to wait for what will seem like a long while before the matter is resolved fully.

BOX 5.8
How to Conduct Yourself During the Hearing

- Respect the formal hearing process even if you believe it to be flawed.
- Dress conservatively and professionally for the hearing.
- Focus in on the fact that your primary role is to present your case against the student. Provide a simple narrative of the facts of the case. Speak deliberately and clearly.
- Adhere scrupulously to any rules of evidence and the procedural rules established for the hearing.
- Refrain from impugning the character of the accused student or any witnesses that he or she may call. Any portrayals or statements that appear to be mean-spirited may work against your case.
- Refrain from reacting in other than a professional manner even if provoked. Keep in mind that *you* are the one who is committed to upholding integrity. Otherwise you would not be here.
- In defending themselves, students may resort to questioning your competence, fair-mindedness, and even your integrity. Should this happen, keep in mind that the worst thing you can do is display rage and counter-attack. Instead, respond thoughtfully to whatever you perceive as a personal assault. If the hearing's procedural rules forbid such personal attacks, remind the hearing board of that.
- Remember that your colleagues sitting on the panel are required to be objective. Therefore, they may strike you as aloof or intimidating in this context. Remind yourself that their demeanor is required. Do not take it personally.
- Close your remarks by thanking the panel for the opportunity to present your case.

- Inform the student of any limits of confidentiality. For example, if the student admits to you that he or she did commit the offense, are you required to inform anyone of this fact?

- Inform the student in as much detail as possible of the nature of your role. The student is likely to be distraught and may perceive your role to be more protective and proactive on your part than it actually is. Refer the student to other resources (e.g., the counseling center) if the student's needs are beyond the limits of your role.

- Ensure that the student has taken advantage of all due process procedures.

- Ensure that the student understands the process, gets all relevant and required materials to the correct office by the proper time, and makes any requests in a timely manner.

- Do not conceive of your role as a defender of what the student may have done. Although you can assist the student in presenting his or her defense to its best effect, you are not normally required, and may not be allowed, to speak for the student or attempt to persuade panel members of the student's innocence.

- If other faculty members question you for appearing to take the student's side against a colleague who had the courage to report a case and go through with it, remind your critics that you are not taking sides. You are helping the process work in the way in which it was designed.

- If you have a role beyond sitting by the student's side during the formal hearing, remain calm and professional at all times. If appropriate and warranted, attempt to assist the student in remaining calm and focused.

SUMMARY

After a brief discussion of students' role in preventing and detecting dishonesty, we suggested a plan for handling cases of suspected dishonesty. In dealing with these cases, it is imperative to follow institutional procedures scrupulously to protect the rights of the student, yourself, and your institution. In the final chapter, we discuss some steps that can be taken at the institutional level to foster academic integrity.

III

Academic Integrity as an Institutional Issue

6

What Institutions Can Do

◆ ◆ ◆

Although the primary purpose of our book has been to assist instructors in understanding and dealing with academic dishonesty, the issues of academic dishonesty and integrity extend beyond the classroom to the institution as a whole (e.g., Alschuler & Blimling, 1995; Gehring & Pavela, 1994; Kibler, 1993b). Therefore, in this chapter, we outline some of the actions that institutions can take to enhance campus-wide academic integrity. We have organized our discussion in terms of the three components of Kibler's (1993b) framework for analyzing the institutional role in fostering academic integrity: establishing an academic integrity policy, implementing an academic integrity program, and developing an academic integrity ethos.

ACADEMIC INTEGRITY POLICY

Because every college and university must develop an academic integrity policy that fits its mission as well as its student body and faculty, we are not going to present a model policy. Rather, we note what we consider to be some of the essential elements of an effective policy. Model policies can be found in various publications (e.g., Kibler et al., 1988; Pavela, 1997a; Risacher & Slonaker, 1996), and the Center for Academic Integrity's (CAI) Web site has a search engine for web pages on integrity policies and honor codes (http://academicintegrity.org/integrity/). Individuals who are not members of CAI may log in and search as guests.

Policy Development

It is a general principle of organizational psychology that people are more likely to adhere to a policy they assist in developing than by policies imposed on them from above (e.g., Cummings & Huse, 1989). It is therefore essential that representatives of all interest groups affected by an institutions academic integrity policy—students, faculty, and student personnel administrators—have a hand in its creation and any subsequent modifications. It is especially important to have student involvement in the policy development process because they are the group who must abide by the policy and who will be subject to any penalties meted out under it. Student input will contribute to student perceptions that the penalties specified by the policy and the procedures by which those penalties are imposed are fair. For those who fear that student involvement may invite a watering down of the provisions, observations by those of us who have worked with student leaders attest to their commitment to a strong policy.

Statement of Policy

An academic integrity policy should begin with a statement informing all members of the institution why the institution values academic integrity and condemns academic dishonesty (see chapt. 1). Although such a statement may seem unnecessary at first glance, people are more likely to comply with rules when they understand the reasons for them (e.g., S. Bok, 1995; Greenberg, 1990). In addition, as Carter (1996) noted, many of today's college students have grown up in a social environment that not only often fails to value integrity but that also sometimes actively disparages it. Therefore, students (and perhaps some faculty members and administrators) may need to be reminded that dishonesty is wrong and that their college or university will take all necessary steps to discourage academic dishonesty and encourage academic integrity.

Specification of Prohibited Behavior

As much as one would like to approach an academic integrity policy in a positive manner, it is probably easier to tell people what is forbidden than what is permitted. Such specification is necessary because, as we noted in Chapter 2, not everyone agrees on all the behaviors that constitute academic dishonesty. The more specifically prohibited behaviors are defined, the easier it is for people to avoid them. For example, the model policy developed by Risacher and Slonaker (1996) defined eight forms of cheating and three forms of plagiarism.

Specification of Responsibilities

To be effective, an academic integrity policy must clearly specify the responsibilities of students, faculty members, and administrators.

Students. The minimum responsibility of students, of course, is to avoid acts of academic dishonesty, but an integrity policy should also remind students of their obligation to actively promote academic integrity. Additional issues should also be considered, such as whether students should be required to report other students' dishonesty when they become aware of it and if so, how they can make a report. For example, will anonymous reports be allowed, such as by means of a telephone "hot line" or unsigned notes placed in an instructor's mailbox?

Faculty Members. Parallel to students' basic responsibility, faculty members' basic responsibility is to conduct their courses in ways that foster academic integrity and inhibit academic dishonesty. But again, additional issues should be considered, such as: Should faculty members be encouraged to have statements concerning academic integrity in their syllabi and to discuss integrity issues in class? If so, what should the content of these statements and discussions be? Should faculty members be required to report *all* instances of academic dishonesty, including those resolved informally if informal resolution is permitted? If not, what guidelines should the instructor use?

Administrators. Administrators are responsible for conducting university business in ways that model a commitment to integrity in all forms (e.g., D. Bok, 1990), thereby encouraging an atmosphere of integrity in their institutions. Such modeling includes making explicit public commitments to integrity, acting in accordance with those statements, and taking appropriate actions on integrity violations by faculty, students, and staff, even if those actions result in embarrassment to the institution. Nothing better demonstrates commitment than taking action at some cost to oneself.

Specification of Resolution Procedures

A very important part of any academic integrity policy is specification of procedures for resolving cases of suspected academic dishonesty. A basic decision to make is whether to allow informal resolution; we noted some of the advantages and disadvantages of this process in chapter 5. If informal resolution is allowed, the policy must specify:

- the exact procedures to be followed, including how the student is to be notified of the suspected dishonesty (preferably in writing),
- what the notification is to say (including a specific description of the suspect behavior and the students right to refuse informal resolution),
- who may be present at meetings between the accusing faculty member and the student (a disinterested witness may be useful),
- actions to take if the student admits or denies the behavior, or accepts the informal offer without admitting guilt, and
- any reporting requirements.

The policy must also specify procedures for formal resolution of allegations of dishonesty. Such procedures usually involve a panel hearing evidence in the case, determining if the student is guilty of an infraction, and if the student is found guilty, assigning a penalty. It is wise to include student members on these panels because students are more likely to perceive a decision as being fair if their peers participate in it. However, formal resolution procedures need not be cumbersome and bureaucratic. Rather, as the University of Maryland's Code of Academic Integrity notes, an integrity hearing "is not in the character of a civil or criminal proceeding. It is not modeled on these adversarial systems; nor does it serve the same social functions. It is not a court or tribunal. Rather it is an academic process unique to the community of scholars that comprise a university" (cited in Pavela & McCabe, 1993, p. 30). Therefore, although a formal hearing must preserve the accused student's right to due process, it does not require all the complex trappings of a civil or criminal trial. Table 6.1 lists the legal requirements for an integrity hearing, the elements of criminal proceedings that are *not* required but that many people assume to be required, and permitted differences from civil and criminal trials. As one state appellate court noted in finding an institution's procedures for resolving allegations of academic dishonesty legally acceptable,

[the student] was served with a written notice of charges; she was made aware of grounds which would justify her expulsion or suspension by way of the student handbook; the hearing tribunal afforded her an opportunity to hear and confront the evidence presented against her and an opportunity to be heard and to offer other evidence if she chose; she was accorded the right to have someone from the college community to assist her in the proceedings; she was informed of the tribunal's finding; she was given access to its decision for her personal review; and finally, she was advised in writing of the discipline imposed. We find that this procedure adequately satisfied due process requirements in a collegial atmosphere. (cited in Gehring & Pavela, 1994, pp. 21–22)

The section of the policy statement dealing with resolution procedures should also emphasize the rights accused students have during both formal and informal resolutions. At a minimum, these rights include

- prohibition of any form of threats or intimidation (although students who ask about the nature of any possible punishments should be given that information);
- a full statement of the evidence in the case (preferably in writing);
- an opportunity to rebut the evidence and to present evidence in their defense, including the testimony of witnesses; and
- the assistance of a faculty member, staff member, administrator or other advisor in preparing and presenting their cases.

Specification of Penalties

As the court noted in the quotation above, an academic integrity policy must specify the penalties that can be imposed for infractions against the policy. If informal resolution is permitted, the policy should clearly state the penalties that instructors are allowed to impose without going through the formal process and the conditions under which they can be imposed (e.g., only when the student admits the infraction). We believe that the maximum punishment that should be allowed under informal resolution is a grade of F or zero on the assignment or test at issue. We think that a more severe penalty should be imposed only when a finding that a student is guilty of academic dishonesty is made by a disinterested party rather than by the affected instructor.

When formal resolution is used, hearing board members must walk a fine line between being too lenient and being too harsh in determining punishments. On the one hand, Pavela and McCabe (1993) held that "The standard penalty for academic dishonesty at many colleges [of] a failing grade on an assignment or in a course . . . trivializes academic dishonesty, and is a weak deterrent, especially for students already in danger of failing the course" (p. 29). On the other hand, Alschuler and Blimling (1995) noted that, "If punishments are too disproportionate to the offense . . .

TABLE 6.1
Formal Resolution: What's Required, What's Not Required, and What's Permitted

Variable	Description
Required	• Written notification to the student of the specific charges • An opportunity for the student to examine the evidence to be presented • At least 10 days notice prior to the hearing • A reasonable effort to accommodate the schedule of any advisor allowed to assist the student • A disinterested hearing board membership (but a superficial knowledge of the case or the people involved is not a disqualification) • Tape recording or transcription of the hearing proceedings • Providing a student found guilty of an infraction with a written explanation of the reasons for the decision • The institution must follow the procedures it establishes
Not Required	• Presence of the student at the hearing if reasonable attempts were made to inform the student of the hearing and if adequate notice was given • A public hearing if the student requests one (although acceding to the request would be a good idea). *Public hearings without the student's permission are not allowed.* • Resolution of any concurrent criminal charges (e.g., breaking and entering to steal a test) prior to the academic dishonesty hearing • Allowing a delay in the hearing without compelling justification • Participation in the proceedings by the student's attorney • Student members on the hearing panel (although it is a good idea) • Proof beyond a reasonable doubt; a preponderance of evidence is sufficient for a guilty finding (although using the intermediate standard of clear and convincing evidence is a good idea) • Warning the student of his or her right to remain silent ("Miranda" rights) • A unanimous finding by the hearing panel; a majority decision is sufficient • A formal appeals process (although it is a good idea)

faculty and students are less likely to report violations" (pp. 124–125). One solution to this problem is to allow a range of possible penalties from which board members can choose based on their view of the severity of the offense.

Pavela and McCabe (1993) recommended the University of Maryland's policy of assigning a grade of "XF" in the course, the "X" indicating that the

TABLE 6.1 (continued)

Variable	Description
Permitted	• "Hearsay" evidence (but it should not be considered sufficient for a guilty finding) • Circumstantial evidence • Consideration of previous offenses or collusion with others when determining penalties • Assigning different penalties for the same offense if the difference is reasonable under the circumstances • Having an administrator make a final determination on the recommendation of a hearing panel rather than having the panel make the final decision • Having an administrator review the proceedings for procedural correctness

Note. Summarized from Kibler et al. (1988, pp. 48–51) and Pavela (1997b).

failure was due to academic dishonesty, which then becomes part of the student's permanent record. As Pavela (1997a) noted,

> [the "XF" grade] represents a compromise between sanctions seen as too lenient (e.g., a reduced grade, which is little or no deterrent to a student already doing poorly in the course) or too harsh (e.g., automatic suspension or expulsion, often regarded by members of hearing panels as being unjust, causing them to distort the fact-finding process to find students "not responsible" in "minor" cases). (p. 107)

Students may petition to have the "X" removed from the transcript after one year if they have committed no further offenses and have successfully completed a noncredit seminar on academic integrity.

One of the shortcomings of most academic integrity policies is that there is no provision for educational sanctions for students judged as guilty of violations. Yet as the University of Maryland policy suggests, a remediation program should be part of any academic integrity policy. A few institutions have developed integrity seminars for first offenders of the academic honesty code. Despite the attractiveness of including live integrity training seminars as a partial or (occasionally) full sanction, they pose logistical, scheduling, and confidentiality dilemmas that may account for the small number of existing programs. Two approaches to integrity training programs are presented in Box 6.1.

Record Keeping

An academic integrity policy should provide for the maintenance of records on students who have admitted to or been found guilty of academic dishonesty. If informal resolution is allowed, these records should also include students who have admitted to academic dishonesty under informal procedures. Such records allow for the identification of repeat offenders who might otherwise fall through the cracks by cheating in a class, admitting it in informal resolution if caught, then doing the same thing in other classes. When these records are kept, the policy could allow the administrator who has oversight of the institution's academic integrity program to institute formal proceedings if a student is reported for more than one informal resolution. A student's academic integrity file would be destroyed after a specified period has elapsed or after the student graduated or left the college or university.

Specification of Prevention Measures

An academic integrity policy should encourage instructors to take measures to reduce students' opportunities to engage in academic dishonesty. For example, a policy might encourage empty chairs between adjacent students during examinations or the use of alternate forms of an exam if spaced seating is not practical. Alternatively, the policy could simply provide a list of countermeasures against academic dishonesty (see chapt. 4) and require instructors to use all that are appropriate to their courses. Regardless of the approach taken, encouraging instructors to use countermeasures reminds them of their responsibilities toward academic integrity.

ACADEMIC INTEGRITY PROGRAM

An academic integrity policy is the basis for an academic integrity program. The program supports the policy by naming a program administrator to oversee implementation of the policy and policy support activities such as

BOX 6.1
Two Approaches to Academic Integrity Seminars

U.S. NAVAL ACADEMY

The Honor Remediation Program at the U.S. Naval Academy (1997) is designed for midshipmen who have violated the honor policy, but are recommended for rehabilitation and put on Honor Probation. The program places a midshipman found in violation of the academy's honor code under the supervision of a faculty mentor who supports and counsels the student, helps the midshipman develop his or her moral reasoning abilities through weekly discussions, and makes a recommendation on the final resolution of the case. As part of the program, the midshipman develops a written plan establishing personal, academic, and professional goals. He or she keeps a journal that documents progress made toward those goals and includes personal notes and reflections on the remediation process. The midshipman must also take part in a community service project for a minimum of 2 hours per week. Finally, the midshipman must submit a 10-page essay in which the midshipman recounts his or her development experience in the remediation program and reflect on the personal and professional meaning of integrity. On recommendation from the mentor, the midshipman may be removed from probation. Although a program of this scope is undoubtedly easier to implement in some academic environments than in others, elements of it can be adapted to most. Visit the U.S. Naval Academy web site at http://www.usna.edu/Admissions/honor.htm (this URL is case-sensitive) for more details about the character development training required of all midshipmen and the remediation program.

MULTIMEDIA INTEGRITY TEACHING TOOL (THE MITT)

The Fund for the Improvement of Postsecondary Education (U.S. Department of Education) supported the development of a computerized integrity seminar at Ball State University. The MITT, designed to be a one-on-one interactive experience with the student and a computer, avoids some of the logistical challenges inherent in live seminars. The MITT's 36 segments cover such topics as why institutions of higher education promote academic integrity, types of academic dishonesty, risks for committing academic dishonesty, and hints for avoiding those risks. The goal is to give students ideas to ponder (especially about themselves and the kind of lives they want to lead), some important information they may have missed along the way, a perspective on the downside of cheating including how others view dishonest people, and the advantages of academic integrity.

Navigating the complete program and passing the content mastery quizzes (and, if assigned, completing a student workbook) takes 8 to 10 hours and can be taken over several sessions. A shorter version (The Little MITT) is also available, consisting of 18 of the more basic lessons. The program keeps track of each student's progress. All or parts of this program can be used as a first-offender educational supplement to other sanctions or in conjunction with an XF grading system, or as part of new student orientation. Visit the MITT web site at http://www.bsu.edu/mitt for a more detailed description of this program and the learning modules.

communication, faculty training, curriculum design, and assistance for faculty members and students.

Program Administration

The academic integrity policy should specify the person who, by virtue of his or her position in the institution, will oversee the implementation of the policy, monitor its effectiveness, recommend changes, keep records, and direct academic integrity program activities. This person is usually an administrator—most often the chief academic affairs officer or chief student affairs officer (Risacher & Slonaker, 1996). She or he should be advised by a committee comprising students, faculty members, and other relevant administrators to ensure that policy decisions reflect the concerns of all constituencies in the institution. The program administrator must also have access to legal advice as needed.

Communication

An essential aspect of any academic integrity program is communication of the academic integrity policy and its implementation to students and faculty. This communication can be accomplished through various documents, discussion forums, articles in the student press, and publication of case outcomes (see Box 6.2).

Documents. The academic integrity policy and procedure process should be published in the documents that are available to all students and faculty members, such as student and faculty handbooks. In addition, it is useful to publish the policy in the college or university catalog. Placing the policy in the catalog makes it available not only to currently enrolled students, but also to prospective students and their parents, thereby emphasizing the importance the institution places on academic integrity. Posting the policy on the college or university's Web site also makes it readily available to students, faculty, and the general public (see http://academicintegrity.org/integrity/ for examples). Faculty members should also include their personal policies, such as that concerning collaboration on assignments, in their syllabi.

Discussions. Because students do not always read handbooks, catalogs, and syllabi, discussions of the academic integrity policy will help students

BOX 6.2
Places Where Academic Policies, Procedures, and General
Information Can Be Publicized

Student handbooks

Institution's catalogs

Institution's site on the World Wide Web

Course syllabi (relevant portions)

Student calendars or other special publications for students

Student newspaper at the beginning of each term

Welcome letter to new students

Posters and book marks

Exam blue books (summary)

Organized discussions

Invited speakers

Electronic bulletin board discussions or presentations of frequently asked questions
    or case summaries

New student orientation

Residence hall discussions

become aware of it. One obvious forum for such discussions is the classroom: On the first day of class, instructors can remind students of the institutional policy, present their own policies, and answer questions. Discussion groups could also be organized in residence halls, student organizations, and, especially, as part of new student orientations. Having students organize and facilitate these discussions could be very useful because their participation would help promote a student norm against academic dishonesty. Finally, an academic integrity policy web page could include a "Frequently Asked Questions" segment in which student and faculty questions and the answers to them could be posted.

The Student Press. The institution's newspaper and other student-run publications can promote knowledge of the academic integrity policy by periodically running articles about it. These articles could be strictly informative, could present student and faculty opinion, and, as discussed next, report the outcomes of cases in which students are accused of academic dishonesty.

Publication of Case Outcomes. People will take an academic integrity policy seriously only if they know it is being enforced. Publication of case outcomes is the best way to ensure that people are aware that suspected violations of the policy are being investigated and students found to have violated the policy are being punished. As Trevino (1990) noted, "disciplining unethical behavior serves an important symbolic purpose, signaling to organizational members that the organization is a just community where norms are upheld and consequences await those who violate them" (p. 207).

Two forums are available for publicizing outcomes. First, the school newspaper could periodically publish summary statistics such as the number of cases, the types of violations alleged, the number of cases in which the student was found to have violated the policy, and the penalties meted out. Occasional case reports, providing more information about the accused student's behavior (but with identifying information omitted), could also be published. A second forum is the World Wide Web: The student honor councils at Rice University and Vanderbilt University post case summaries on their web pages.

Special Programs and Activities. In our experience, some students can become intrigued with academic integrity issues and are willing to get involved in promoting it. With the help of an interested administrator or faculty member, this interest can lead to campus projects and programs designed to help publicize and raise awareness of the importance of academic integrity.

Some examples of special projects that have been brought to our attention include the creation of a colorful, eye-catching series of posters with slogans espousing the benefits of honesty and the disadvantages of dishonesty; a film series (followed by discussions) of films illustrating profound ethical themes (e.g., *Quiz Show*, *White Squall*, and *Casualties of War*); and a seminar series for student leaders on the critical role they can play in creating a climate of integrity on campus. We have also seen publications of the results of surveys on campus attitudes toward cheating on web pages and in school newspapers. Because the vast majority of college students see upholding academic integrity as important and disapprove of cheating and those students who engage in it (despite the irony that the majority of them may have also engaged in it at least once), the results may create a positive norming effect for the student body.

Faculty Training

As noted in chapter 1, college and university faculty members rarely receive training on how to prevent, control, and confront academic dishonesty. Therefore, such training—covering the types of information included in this book—is an important part of any academic integrity program. This training could take the form of a combination of written materials explaining institutional policies and procedures, symposia that provide clarification of points of policy and procedure that faculty have difficulty with, and small-group discussions of cases illustrating gray areas.

We encourage such training for all newly hired graduate teaching assistants and faculty members, and refresher training can be offered periodically for all instructors. Such training is especially important for graduate students who teach their own courses. Kerkvliet and Sigmund (1999) found that students were much more likely to cheat on exams in classes taught by graduate students than in those taught by more experienced instructors.

In addition, an Academic Integrity Newsletter could be published to provide new information and a forum in which faculty members could exchange helpful hints. Universities should also provide training on academic integrity issues for graduate students who plan on college and university teaching careers. Providing such training not only educates instructors about the problem and how to deal with it, but sends the message that the campus is concerned and expects its members to be actively involved in maintaining high educational standards.

Assistance to Faculty Members

In addition to training faculty members on academic integrity issues, institutions must support them in their efforts to establish and maintain high standards of integrity in their classes. Kibler (1993b) recommended that institutions implement the following assistance strategies:

- Provide proctoring services for tests as needed. It is extremely difficult for instructors to monitor exams in larger classes without assistance. Maintaining a pool of student proctors is highly desirable in those institutions offering large classes.

• Provide case assistance and consultation services for faculty members when violations occur, including information on policy, guidance in how to correctly follow procedures, expectations, methods for gathering evidence, and strategies for presenting evidence in hearings.

• Appoint an experienced faculty member in each department to be the department's Academic Integrity Liaison to provide advice and assistance to colleagues.

• Provide recognition for faculty members who properly handle cases of academic dishonesty. Such recognition need not be elaborate. For example, Gehring and Pavela (1994) suggested that "Even a simple letter of appreciation, signed by the academic dean or vice president and placed in the faculty member's file, will be at least some acknowledgement of the time and energy which the faculty member devoted to the matter" (p. 31).

As noted in chapter 1, instructors who feel unsupported by administrators are extremely reluctant to confront students suspected of academic dishonesty. Horror stories abound about administrators who abandon instructors who have the courage to pursue cases of academic dishonesty. These stories are passed across the country by word of mouth and on the Internet, and occasionally they are reported in professional publications (e.g., Schneider, 1999; Wilson, 1998). It is important for administrators to make it as comfortable as possible for faculty members to fulfill their duty to maintain integrity. Department chairs, especially, can play an important role in encouraging faculty to maintain academic integrity in the classroom and to support those who detect and confront it. For example, because instructors may be concerned that teaching evaluations will suffer if a student in the class is accused of dishonesty, a policy could be established to ignore the lowest evaluation in a class in which an accusation of dishonesty was made. Ideally, one would ignore only the accused student's evaluation, but such a procedure would make anonymous evaluations impossible. Box 6.3 provides an example of the positive effects that administrative support can have on both faculty and students.

Assistance to Students

Students as well as faculty members need assistance in maintaining academic integrity. The communication and training strategies described previously are steps in this direction, but other measures are also possible. For example, the results of Whitley's (1998) review of factors associated with academic dishonesty suggest the following: Students who are likely to engage in academic dishonesty are deficient in study skills, lower in

BOX 6.3
The Supportive Role of Administrators

The investigation of a case of homework cheating in my Ethics class led to the discovery of systematic abuses, including the theft of student work from campus computers. When initially confronted, the student involved fully expected me to simply let him redo the assignment or, at worst, give him a zero on it. His complacency alarmed me, so I asked the Dean to speak with him. That conversation led to a deeper administrative investigation, which eventually uncovered a small network of habitual cheaters who expected little, if any, punishment for their actions. The willingness of the Academic Dean and the Dean of Students to pursue this matter allowed me to concentrate on my teaching. Best of all, however, the honest students were so encouraged by the knowledge that something would be done to cheaters that they reported another incident directly to the Dean shortly thereafter. The expectation of academic honesty must be backed up by a willingness to enforce it for the teaching and learning process to thrive on college campuses. (Heather Reid, Morningside College, interview with Bernard Whitley, March 1999)

industriousness, and higher in procrastination and test anxiety than students who are less likely to cheat.

Aggressive publication of the availability of support services such as learning centers and resources such as tutors, writing advisors, and study skill counselors will help ensure that students who feel in need of assistance can obtain it. Furthermore, faculty members should be actively encouraged to refer students to those services. In some cases, students might be well served by psychological counseling (e.g., students whose cheating appears to be at least partially caused by anxiety or major life stressors). Although you cannot mandate that a student seek such counseling, information about available services available can be discussed in class and publicized campus-wide.

Deficiencies in study skills and industriousness could lead students to perceive even a normal academic work load as unusually heavy—another factor associated with academic dishonesty. Academic advisors should be sensitive to students who complain about being overworked and consider advising those students to take reduced course loads and referring them to sources of assistance for their problems. Finally, because poor study quality is related to academic dishonesty and because student housing is often noisy and so not conducive to effective study, institutions should consider establishing quiet study areas in residence halls and strictly enforcing the rules governing them. In areas where risk of criminal victimization may inhibit students from using the library as a study site at night, institutions could establish escort services that operate between the library and residence halls and parking lots.

As noted in chapter 2, international students from some cultures may not be aware of what behaviors the European cultural tradition defines as academic dishonesty. In some cases, behaviors that are acceptable or normative in the students' home cultures, such as excessive collaboration on exams, may violate Western academic norms. For example, one professor told us of three students who openly traded exam score sheets among themselves. The astonished instructor approached them to ask what they thought they were doing. One replied, "Just helping each other. We all want to do the best we possibly can." In a private meeting, the students explained in a matter of fact manner how friends are required to assist each other in any way possible. They were surprised that their exam behavior posed any problem.

Orientation programs for international students should include an overview of the European view of academic integrity. The use of specific examples and cases discussions will help these students develop a hands-on feel for what is permitted and what is forbidden. We found that the perspective outlined in Box 6.4 provides a useful starting point.

Creating Momentum for Integrity Programs

We have heard colleagues from around the country say that it takes enthusiastic support from the administration, or at least a large and influential group of colleagues, to produce any change in matters relating to academic integrity. Even if change begins, the pessimistic viewpoint holds, years will pass before a noticeable difference can be seen. This view is often used to justifying inaction and uninvolvement.

We believe that even one member of the campus community can make a difference, and that change need not take years to show its effects. This person must, of course, be very committed, persevere when the inevitable roadblocks present themselves, and search early on for others who have an interest in academic integrity. Those who are enthusiastic without appearing arrogant or rigidly self-righteous are the most likely to succeed. Students may seem like an unlikely source of support and involvement, but they may

BOX 6.4
A Perspective on Educating International Students About Western Definitions of Academic Integrity

It may be difficult to ever create guidelines specific to academic dishonesty for international students because much of what we think of as academic integrity is based on very specific definitions for things like achievement, individual work, and independent thought.

What I usually do with incoming international students is give them some tips for understanding why things happen the way they do in an American classroom. This discussion dovetails into a larger discussion of fundamental cultural idiosyncrasies in the United States. If students understand the premium that Americans place on individuality, hard work, independent achievement, and the right to privacy, they then have the tools to deal with the myriad situations that will present themselves in the classroom. This continual sort of orientation seems to be functional in most cases.

I also let students know that if they are ever in doubt about appropriate behavior, they should talk to me or the instructor. It takes a while for international students to believe that professors are approachable because this is also an idiosyncrasy of higher education in the United States, found almost nowhere else in the world.

—Sue Mennicke, Director of Study Abroad and International Student Services
  Southwestern University

Note. (personal communication, January 14, 1999, with permission.)

prove to be among the most helpful especially if activities can be structured in ways that help them achieve some of their own goals. Box 6.5 offers an example of a campus pioneer who gathered support, slowly at first, but ultimately to effect major changes in shifting her institution from being indifferent to academic integrity to being actively dedicated to maintaining a climate of academic integrity.

ETHOS PROMOTING ACADEMIC INTEGRITY

Campus Life—In Search of Community, published by the Carnegie Foundation for the Advancement of Teaching (1990), proposed six general principles that, taken together, define the kind of community that every college and university should strive to become:

BOX 6.5
The Power of One

A colleague once told Dr. Lisa Gray-Shellberg, Professor of Psychology at California State University, Dominguez Hills, that her greatest weakness was an excess of hope. She responded by reciting her three working principles: good ideas will have their day, just try again when faced with obstacles, and join up with like-minded others. Gray-Shellberg had a long-standing interest in academic integrity and had been concerned because resources beyond a basic institutional honesty code printed in the university's catalog were not readily available. Her initial attempts to move her university toward a more active involvement in academic integrity projects were quickly dismissed because the administration already saw itself as having enough problems without taking on any new ones.

She then started talking informally to colleagues, including the Director of Student Development, and found a few who shared her interests and concerns. Slowly a group came together. A series of messages on such topics as "What can faculty do to promote academic integrity?" and "What are the options when students are caught cheating?" were devised and sent to the entire faculty by e-mail. The group worked on an introductory statement to the honesty policy and, over some objections from unlikely places, prevailed. The result was a full page devoted to the central place of academic integrity in the campus community. One member of the group developed an excellent and informative page to add to the campus web site. The group also did some research, including an analysis of class syllabi. The initial findings were that only 3% of the syllabi sampled contained any statement about cheating. Within 3 years, however, the campus policy requires that statements about academic integrity policy *must* be in every syllabus.

Gray-Shellberg also focused her own scholarly research activity on academic integrity, involving a great many of her students in the process. She and her students have given a number of papers at regional and professional meetings. She reports that a paradigm shift has occurred on her campus with the realization that academic dishonesty causes everyone to suffer, and that every member of the campus community has a responsibility to actively deal with it.

• A college or university is an *educationally purposeful community*, a place where faculty and students share academic goals and work together to strengthen teaching and learning on the campus.

• A college or university is an *open community*, a place where freedom of expression is uncompromisingly protected and where civility is powerfully affirmed.

• A college or university is a *just community*, a place where the sacredness of the person is honored and where diversity is aggressively pursued.

- A college or university is a *disciplined community*, a place where individuals accept their obligations to the group and where well-defined governance procedures guide behavior for the common good.

- A college or university is a *caring community*, a place where the well-being of each member is sensitively supported and where service to others is encouraged.

- A college or university is a *celebratory community*, one in which the heritage of the institution is remembered and where rituals affirming both tradition and change are widely shared. (p. 7)

The nature and feel of the campus community environment—the campus ethos—is a powerful influence on individual students' attitudes toward cheating. If students perceive their campus as merely providing a means to an end, and as unjust, disjointed, laissez faire, impersonal, and without a core identity, deterrents to cheating may be very weak.

In this section we briefly discuss the core of the strategy for promoting academic integrity—development of an academic integrity ethos. An academic integrity ethos reflects an institutional value system that "coveys that academic integrity is something to revere, honor and uphold" (Kibler, 1993b, p. 12). Such an ethos focuses on developing individuals who place a high value on integrity and behave ethically because their personal value systems demand it rather than because organizational rules compel it (Paine, 1994).

Students as well as faculty members and administrators recognize the importance of a campus culture that actively encourages academic integrity. When McCabe et al. (1999) asked students what could be done to improve academic integrity on their campuses, among their suggestions were that moral and ethical socialization be part of the educational process and that students be encouraged to know and abide by the rules of proper conduct.

In her discussion of organizational integrity, Paine (1994) suggested that there are two approaches that an organization can take in promoting ethical behavior: a rule compliance strategy and an integrity strategy. As shown in Table 6.2, a rule compliance strategy for academic integrity emphasizes the establishment and enforcement of rules for behavior, and so comprises the processes of policy and program development that we have discussed. But as Paine (1994) noted,

An integrity strategy is broader, deeper, and more demanding than a [rule] compliance initiative. Broader in that it seeks to enable responsible conduct. Deeper in that

TABLE 6.2
Compliance and Integrity as Institutional Strategies for Dealing With Academic Dishonesty

Characteristics of Compliance Strategy		Characteristics of Integrity Strategy	
Ethos	Conformity with externally imposed standards	Ethos	Self-regulation according to chosen standards
Objective	Prevent academic dishonesty	Objective	Promote responsible behavior
Leadership	Lawyer-driven	Leadership	Jointly driven by students, faculty, and student personnel administrators with the advice of lawyers
Methods	Education, behavior control, penalties	Methods	Education, leadership, personal accountability, social controls, behavior control, penalties, rehabilitation
Behavioral assumptions	Autonomous beings guided by self-interest	Behavioral assumptions	Social beings guided by self-interest, values, ideals, peers

it cuts to the ethos and operating systems of the organization and its members, their guiding values and patterns of thought and action. And more demanding in that it requires an active effort to define the responsibilities and aspirations that constitute an organization's ethical compass. (p. 111)

Elements of an Integrity Ethos

A number of writers have discussed the need for an *academic integrity ethos*, although not always using that term (e.g., Alschuler & Blimling, 1995; Gehring & Pavela, 1994; Kibler, 1993b; Pavela & McCabe, 1993). We propose four elements of an academic integrity ethos: institutional integrity, a learning-oriented environment, a values-based curriculum, and an

TABLE 6.2 (continued)

Implementation of Compliance Strategy		Implementation of Integrity Strategy	
Standards	Institutional rules, criminal and civil law	*Standards*	Institutional values and aspirations; social obligations, including law
Staffing	Student personnel administrators, lawyers	*Staffing*	Students, faculty, and student personnel administrators advised by lawyers
Activities	Develop institutional rules, communicate rules, investigate rule violations, enforce rules	*Activities*	Develop institutional values, communicate and teach values, model values, integrate values education into the curriculum, provide advice and assistance, assess values performance, identify and resolve problems, oversee compliance activities
Education	What the rules are and how they are enforced	*Education*	Ethical decision making: what the rules are and how they are enforced

Note. From "Managing for Organizational Integrity" by Lynn Sharp Paine, March-April 1994. Copyright 1994 by the President and Fellows of Harvard College. Reprinted by permission of *Harvard Business Review.*

honor code. We recognized that, with the exception of institutional integrity, it might not be possible to implement all aspects of these elements in all colleges and universities. However, we do encourage all institutions to do as much as possible to implement them.

Institutional Integrity. Because respect or a lack of respect for integrity as a value is an aspect of the overall culture of an organization (e.g., Paine,

1994; Trevino, 1990), academic institutions cannot foster academic integrity in isolation from other aspects of institutional integrity. Unless the leadership and representatives of the institution enforce integrity in all areas of the institution's functioning, public statements, business affairs, athletics, research, and so forth, neither faculty, students, nor the general public will believe that the institution has a valid commitment to academic integrity. As Gehring and Pavela (1994) noted, "misleading statements in institutional publications, or fraud and abuse in campus athletic programs, will make a mockery of official pronouncements encouraging the student body as a whole to adhere to high standards of academic integrity" (p. 29).

A Learning-Oriented Environment. Eison, Pollio, and Milton (1986) posited that students can take two orientations toward education: Those who have a learning orientation are motivated by a desire to acquire new information and ideas that will enhance their personal and professional development, whereas those who have a grade orientation are motivated by a desire to achieve high grades regardless of whether they learn anything of significance. Similarly, we believe, educational institutions can take two orientations toward educating students: a learning orientation or a product orientation. Learning-oriented institutions evaluate their success in terms of student learning and intellectual development; product-oriented institutions are more concerned with quantity: the number of students "processed," the amount of grant money obtained by faculty, the amount of revenue generated by the athletic program, and so forth.

Just as learning-oriented faculty can foster academic integrity in their classrooms by showing respect for their students and care for their education (see chap. 3), learning-oriented institutions can foster academic integrity in the student body as a whole by showing the same care and respect (e.g., Pavela & McCabe, 1993). Learning-oriented institutions are typically characterized by small class sizes, curricular and extracurricular activities focusing on the personal and intellectual development of their students, and an atmosphere of collegiality and mutual respect among students, faculty members, administrators, and staff members. Although environmental factors can have a strong influence on the extent to which an institution must take some degree of product orientation (such as when funding for a public institution is dependent on its enrollment), other aspects of the orientation (such as the relative importance given to academics and athletics) are less externally constrained. In addition, even institutions that are forced to have large classes to compensate for inadequate funding can allocate the resources that are available to programs that enhance student learning.

A Values-Oriented Curriculum. Just as academic integrity is only one part of an institutional value system, it is only one part of an individual's value system. Therefore, students' academic integrity is most effectively fostered in an academic environment that encourages their overall moral development. Carter (1996) noted that a basic aspect of integrity is thinking about whether an action is right or wrong before deciding on whether to take the action. Because ethical thinking, like other aspects of critical thinking, is best developed through practice, institutions should make ethical decision making a central part of their curricula. For example, institutions could require an ethics course as part of their core curricula, require all courses to include discussions of the ethical issues relevant to the course topic, or make a departmental course in professional ethics a graduation requirement (or, ideally, institute all of these policies). In addition, the institution could sponsor speakers on ethical issues and encourage departmental colloquia on ethics by offering supplemental funding for them. Examples of such institution-wide programs are published annually in the John Templeton Foundation's *Honor Roll for Character-Building Colleges* (e.g., John Templeton Foundation, 1997).

An Honor Code. Establishment of an honor code is the clearest statement that a college or university can make that it values and is committed to academic integrity. Honor codes have four distinguishing characteristics (Melendez, 1985):

- *Unproctored examinations.* A uniform requirement that academic honesty in a final examination be enforced only by the voluntary cooperation of each student being examined.
- *Pledge.* A signed statement required from each student that he or she will act or has acted honorably in the preparation of work to be accepted for academic credit or evaluation.
- *Reportage.* An obligation placed upon each student not to tolerate any infraction of honor by a fellow member of the community.
- *Court.* A peer judiciary whose primary concern is the infraction of honor by students. A "peer judiciary" means a body with investigative or disciplinary powers where (1) a student serves as chairperson, (2) student membership comprises a majority of the body, or (3) student consent is necessary or sufficient to change the constitution of the body. (cited in Pavela & McCabe, 1993, p. 30)

Honor codes, like academic integrity policies, must be tailored to the college or university to which they pertain. Consequently, their content varies considerably from institution to institution. As we noted at the beginning of this chapter, the Center for Academic Integrity provides a search engine for locating honor codes available on the World Wide Web (http:///academicintegrity.org/integrity/).

As Pavela and McCabe (1993) noted, honor codes are not a panacea for an institution's academic integrity problems. An honor code is a reflection of the institution's integrity ethos; it is not the ethos itself. Consequently, the institution of an honor code will have no effect unless the institution's students, faculty, and administration already have a commitment to integrity (e.g., D. Bok, 1990). Therefore, implementation of an honor code should probably be the final, rather than an initial, step in developing an institutional integrity ethos.

Developing an Academic Integrity Ethos

Development of an academic integrity ethos requires changing the culture of the institution. In some cases this will be a large change, in others a small change, depending on the starting point. In either case, it will entail a well-designed, coordinated organization development effort (e.g., Trevino, 1990) and so should be conducted by experts in that field. However, we would like to make three points in this regard.

Leadership From the Top. Change must have the clear support of institutional leaders. Schein (1985) suggested that there are at least three ways in which leaders influence organizational culture. First, members of an organization are going to see as important the things to which leaders pay attention, measure, and control. For example, if the president of an institution and faculty and student governance groups request periodic reports on academic integrity issues, then members of the institution will place more importance on academic integrity than in the absence of such interest. Second, leaders' reactions to critical incidents reveal cultural values. For example, if a star athlete is caught cheating on an exam and the president makes excuses rather than takes corrective action, the true value placed on academic integrity at that institution becomes unmistakably clear. Similarly, if faculty, administrators, or staff members who commit scientific or other serious forms of misconduct are protected or dealt with superficially, commitment to integrity will be viewed as mere window dressing. Finally, leaders both consciously and (as in the last examples) unconsciously model behaviors and make policy statements that members of the institution use as a basis for their own behavior. To the extent that leaders' behavior and statements model and support academic integrity, others will follow.

The Need for Systemic Change. Any change effort designed to foster an academic integrity ethos must encompass the entire institutional system, not focus on only one aspect of it. As noted earlier, the academic integrity of an educational institution reflects its overall ethical health, so a change effort must focus on all members of the institution: students, faculty, administrators, and staff in all their institutional activities (e.g., teaching, learning, business, athletics, etc.). Omission of any group or activity leaves a hole in the institutional integrity framework that weakens the entire structure.

The Need for a Long-Term Perspective. Changing an organization's culture is neither quick nor easy (e.g., Trevino, 1990). Therefore, our final point is that if an institution decides to develop an academic integrity ethos, its members must take the long view and be prepared to accept and overcome temporary setbacks as well as make progress toward becoming a community that values and fosters both personal and institutional integrity. The Center for Academic Integrity (CAI) provides opportunities to learn what other institutions are doing in these regards. See Box 6.6 for more information about the CAI. Another important resource is the American College Personnel Association's Commission on Campus Judicial Affairs and Legal Issues, described in Box 6.7.

As Wilcox and Ebbs (1992) reminded us, higher education has no external certification requirements for its professional staff because, in the beginning, people had faith that the commitment of colleges and universities to high moral standards was unquestionable. Although the face of higher education has changed considerably over the years, the responsibility for maintaining high standards of moral conduct and the powers to investigate and sanction those who violate those standards remain, for the most part, internal processes.

Accounts of high-level administrators covering up or white-washing incidents of serious misconduct among faculty, athletes, and other administrators are commonplace and contribute to cynicism among all members of the academic community. Courageous administrators who confront the

BOX 6.6
The Center for Academic Integrity (CAI)

Institutions of higher education can join a national network of colleges and universities concerned with academic integrity issues. The Center for Academic Integrity (CAI) is associated with the Keenan Ethics Program at Duke University and provides a forum to identify and promote the values of academic integrity. Research is encouraged and supported, and successful approaches to enhancing academic integrity are showcased. The organization is also working on the Fundamental Principles Project that will attempt to define the level of integrity expected of all students in their academic work. CAI holds an annual meeting in late fall to which judicial affairs staff and other interested administrators and staff, faculty, and students are welcome.

Visit the CAI web page at http://academicintegrity.org/. For more information about the CAI, write to Diane M. Waryold, Executive Director, The Center for Academic Integrity, Box 90434, Duke University, Durham, NC 27709; e-mail: dmwaryol@duke.edu.

ethical or conduct violations within their organization immediately and forthrightly may not be newsworthy because we do not hear about them very often. Recognizing that the administration sets the mark for the integrity level to which they should aspire, those who put the high ideals expressed in institutional mission statements into effect deserve public praise and recognition.

SUMMARY

We conclude our book with suggestions concerning what institutions can do to enhance academic integrity. All institutions should have academic integrity policies. These policies should state the institutional position on academic integrity and specify what behaviors are prohibited; the responsibilities of faculty, students, and administrators; procedures for resolving suspected cases of academic dishonesty and the penalties for dishonesty; how records are to be kept; and the measures that can be taken to prevent academic dishonesty on academic exercises. An academic integrity program goes beyond the mere statement of policy to address issues of communication of the policy, faculty training, curriculum design, and

BOX 6.7
The American College Personnel Association

Commission XV (Campus Judicial Affairs Legal Issues) of The American College Personnel Association has many active programs related to legal rights and responsibilities within the academic community. This group provides support and information about legal issues, suggests ways to contribute to individual and group responsibility, and seeks to stimulate implementation of judicial programs consistent with educational principles. More information about the Commission can be found at its web site (http//www.judprog.uga.edu/acpaxv.nsf), which contains procedural manuals, assessment instruments, and ideas for prevention and disciplinary programs that may be downloaded.

assistance to faculty and students. Institutions should also strive to develop an ethos that promotes academic integrity by emphasizing institutional integrity, learning-oriented environments, and values-oriented curricula. Changing an institutional culture in this way is difficult, but the results are worth the effort involved.

References

◆◆◆

Aiken, L. R. (1991). Detecting, understanding, and controlling for cheating on tests. *Research in Higher Education, 32,* 725–736.

Ajzen, I. (1991). The theory of planned behavior. *Organizational Behavior and Human Decision Processes, 50,* 179–211.

Alschuler, A. S., & Blimling, G. S. (1995). Curbing epidemic cheating through systemic change. *College Teaching, 43,* 123–125.

Anderman, E. M., Griesinger, T., & Westerfeld, G. (1998). Motivation and cheating during early adolescence. *Journal of Educational Psychology, 90,* 84–93.

Anderson, M. (1992). *Impostors in the temple.* New York: Simon & Schuster.

Baldwin, D. C., Jr., Daugherty, S.R., Rowley, B. D., & Schwarz, M. R. (1996). Cheating in medical school: A survey of second-year students at 31 schools. *Academic Medicine, 71,* 267–273.

Barnett, D. C., & Dalton, J. C. (1981). Why college students cheat. *Journal of College Student Personnel, 22,* 545–551.

Bellezza, F. S., & Bellezza, S. F. (1989). Detection of cheating on multiple-choice tests by using error-similarity analysis. *Teaching of Psychology, 16,* 151–155.

Benning, V. (1998, October 4). High-tech cheating hits the campus: Computers make it easy for college students to break rules. *Washington Post,* p. A01.

Berthold, K. A., & Hoover, J. H. (2000). Correlates of bullying and victimization among intermediate school students in the Midwestern USA. *School Psychology International, 21,* 65–78.

Blankenship, K. L., & Whitley, B. E., Jr. (2000). Relation of general deviance to academic dishonesty. *Ethics & Behavior, 10,* 1–12.

Bloom, B. S. (1984). The 2-sigma problem: The search for methods of group instruction as effective as one-to-one tutoring. *Educational Researcher, 13*(6), 4–16.

Bok, D. (1990). *Universities and the future of America.* Durham, NC: Duke University Press.

Bok, S. (1995). *Common values.* Columbia: University of Missouri Press.

Bresnock, A. E., Graves, P. E., & White, N. (1989). Multiple-choice testing: Question and response position. *Journal of Economic Education, 20,* 239–245.

Brickman, W. W. (1961). Ethics, examinations, and education. *School and Society, 89,* 412–415.

Brown, B. S. (1995). The academic ethics of graduate business students: A survey. *Journal of Education for Business, 70,* 151–156.

Bushway, A., & Nash, W. R. (1977). School cheating behavior. *Review of Educational Research, 47,* 623–632.

Bushweller, K. (1999). Generation of cheaters. *American School Board Journal, 186*(4), 24–32.

Cahn, S. M. (1994). *Saints and scamps: Ethics in academia.* Lanham, MD: Rowman & Littlefield.

Carnegie Foundation for the Advancement of Teaching. (1990). *Campus life: In search of community.* Princeton, NJ: Author.

Carnevale, D. (1999, November 12). How to proctor from a distance. *Chronicle of Higher Education,* pp. A47–A48.

Carter, S. L. (1996). *Integrity.* New York: HarperCollins.

Cizek, G. J. (1999). *Cheating on tests: How to do it, detect it, prevent it.* Mahwah, NJ: Lawrence Erlbaum Associates.

Cohen, J. (1992). A power primer. *Psychological Bulletin, 112,* 155–159.

Cole, S., & McCabe, D. L. (1996). Issues in academic integrity. In W. L. Mercer (Ed.), *Critical issues in judicial affairs: Current trends in practice* (pp. 67–77). San Francisco, Jossey-Bass.

Collison, M. (1990, January 17). Apparent rise in students' cheating has college officials worried. *Chronicle of Higher Education,* p. A33.

157

Connell, C. (1981). Term paper mills continue to grind. *Educational Record, 62*(3), 19–28.

Corbett, B. (1999). *The cheater's handbook*. New York: Regan Books.

Cordeiro, W. P. (1995). Should a school of business change its ethics to conform to the cultural diversity of its students? *Journal of Education for Business, 71*, 27–29.

Cummings, T. G., & Huse, E. F. (1989). *Organization development and change* (4th ed.). St. Paul, MN: West.

Dalton, J. C. (Ed.). (1985). *Promoting values development in college students*. Washington, DC: National Association of Student Personnel Administrators.

Davis, K. (1992). Student cheating: A defensive essay. *English Journal, 81*(6), 72–74.

Davis, S. F., Grover, C. A., Becker, A. H., & McGregor, L. N. (1992). Academic dishonesty: Prevalence, determinants, techniques, and punishments. *Teaching of Psychology, 19*, 16–20.

Davis, S. F., & Ludvigson, H. W. (1995). Additional data on academic dishonesty and a proposal for remediation. *Teaching of Psychology, 22*, 119–121.

Davis, S. F., Noble, L. M., Zak, E. N., & Dreyer, K. K. (1994). A comparison of cheating and learning/grade orientation in American and Australian college students. *College Student Journal, 28*, 353–356.

Deckert, G. D. (1993). Perspectives on plagiarism from ESL students in Hong Kong. *Journal of Second Language Writing, 2*, 131–148.

Diekhoff, G. M., LaBeff, E. E., Clark, R. E., Williams, L. E., Francis, B., & Haines, V. J. (1996). College cheating: Ten years later. *Research in Higher Education, 37*, 487–502.

Drum, A. (1987). Responding to plagiarism. *College Composition and Communication, 37*, 241–243.

Dwyer, D. J., & Hecht, J. B. (1996). Using statistics to catch cheaters: Methodological and legal issues for student personnel administrators. *NASPA Journal, 33*, 125–135.

Eison, J. A., Pollio, H. R., & Milton, O. (1986). Educational and personal characteristics of four different types of learning- and grade-oriented students. *Contemporary Educational Psychology, 11*, 54–67.

Erickson, B. L., & Strommer, D. W. (1991). *Teaching college freshmen*. San Francisco: Jossey-Bass.

Fass, R. A. (1990). Cheating and plagiarism. In W. M. May (Ed.), *Ethics and higher education* (pp. 170–183). New York: Macmillan.

Faulkender, P. J., Range, L. M., Hamilton, M., Strehlow, M., Jackson, S., Blanchard, E., & Dean, P. (1994). The case of the stolen psychology test: An analysis of an actual cheating incident. *Ethics & Behavior, 4*, 209–217.

Fitzgerald, J. (1987). Research on revision in writing. *Review of Educational Research, 57*, 481–506.

Franklyn-Stokes, A., & Newstead, S. E. (1995). Undergraduate cheating: Who does what and why? *Studies in Higher Education, 20*(2), 39–52.

Frary, R. B. (1992, April). *Statistical detection of multiple-choice test answer copying: State of the art*. Paper presented at the annual meeting of the Measurement Services Association, San Francisco. (ERIC Document Reproduction Service No. ED 351 358)

Gardner, W. M., Roper, J. T., Gonzalez, C. C., & Simpson, R. G. (1988). Analysis of cheating on academic assignments. *Psychological Record, 38*, 543–555.

Gehring, D. (1998). When institutions and their faculty address issues of academic dishonesty: Realities and myths. In D. D. Barnett, L. Rudolph, & K. O. Clifford (Eds.), *Academic integrity matters* (pp. 77–92). Washington, DC: National Association of Student Personnel Administrators.

Gehring, D., & Pavela, G. (1994). *Issues and perspectives on academic integrity* (2nd ed.). Washington, DC: National Association of Student Personnel Administrators.

Genereaux, R. L., & McLeod, B. A. (1995). Circumstances surrounding cheating: A questionnaire study of college students. *Research in Higher Education, 36*, 687–704.

Glick, D., & Turque, B. (1993, September 27). Sailing through troubled seas. *Newsweek, 126*, p. 44.

Gohmann, S. F., & Spector, L. C. (1989). Test scrambling and student performance. *Journal of Economic Education, 20*, 235–238.

Goldsmith, H. (1998). The impact of technology on academic integrity. In D. D. Barnett, L. Rudolph, & K. O. Clifford (Eds.), *Academic integrity matters* (pp. 135–141). Washington, DC: National Association of Student Personnel Administrators.

Graham, M. A., Monday, J., O'Brien, K., & Steffen, S. (1994). Cheating at small colleges: An examination of student and faculty attitudes and behaviors. *Journal of College Student Development, 35,* 255–260.

Greenberg, J. (1990). Employee theft as a reaction to underpayment inequity: The hidden costs of pay cuts. *Journal of Applied Psychology, 75,* 561–568.

Greenberg, J. (1993). Stealing in the name of justice: Informational and interpersonal moderators of theft reactions to underpayment inequity. *Organizational Behavior and Human Decision Processes, 54,* 81–103.

Gronlund, N. E. (1993). *How to make achievement tests and assessments* (5th ed.). Boston: Allyn & Bacon.

Guernsey, L. (1998, December 11). Web site will check papers against data base to detect plagiarism. *Chronicle of Higher Education,* p. A38.

Hardy, R. J. (1981). Preventing academic dishonesty: Some important tips for political science professors. *Teaching Political Science, 9,* 68–77.

Heisler, G. (1974). Ways to deter law violators: Effects of level of threat and vicarious punishment on cheating. *Journal of Consulting and Clinical Psychology, 42,* 577–582.

Hendershott, A., Drinan, P. F., & Cross, M. (1999). Gender and academic integrity. *Journal of College Student Development, 40,* 345–354.

Hickman, J. N. (1998, March 23). Cybercheats. *The New Republic, 218,* 14–15.

Hindman, C. D. (1980). Crib notes in the classroom: Cheaters never win. *Teaching of Psychology, 7,* 166–168.

Hollinger, R. C., & Lanza-Kaduce, L. (1996). Academic dishonesty and the perceived effectiveness of countermeasures: An empirical survey of cheating at a major public university. *NASPA Journal, 33,* 292–306.

Houston, J. P. (1976). Amount and loci of classroom answer copying, spaced seating, and alternate test forms. *Journal of Educational Psychology, 68,* 729–735.

Houston, J. P. (1977). Cheating: The illusory edge. *Contemporary Educational Psychology, 2,* 364–372.

Houston, J. P. (1978). Curvilinear relationships among anticipated success, cheating behavior, temptation to cheat, and perceived instrumentality of cheating. *Journal of Educational Psychology, 70,* 758–762.

Houston, J. P. (1983). College classroom cheating, threat, sex, and prior performance. *College Student Journal, 17,* 196–235.

Houston, J. P. (1986a). Classroom answer copying: Roles of acquaintanceship and free vs. assigned seating. *Journal of Educational Psychology, 78,* 230–232.

Houston, J. P. (1986b). Survey corroboration of experimental findings on classroom cheating behavior. *College Student Journal, 20,* 168–173.

Houston, J. P., & Ziff, T. (1976). Effects of success and failure on cheating behavior. *Journal of Educational Psychology, 68,* 371–376.

Hu, W., & Grove, C. L. (1991). *Encountering the Chinese: A guide for Americans.* Yarmouth, ME: Intercultural Press.

Jendrek, M. P. (1989). Faculty reactions to academic dishonesty. *Journal of College Student Development, 30,* 401–406.

Jendrek, M. P. (1992). Students' reactions to academic dishonesty. *Journal of College Student Development, 33,* 260–273.

Jewler, A. J., Gardner, J. N., & McCarthy, M. J. (1993). *Your college experience: Strategies for success.* Belmont, CA: Wadsworth.

Johnston, D. K. (1996). Cheating: Limits of individual integrity. *Journal of Moral Education, 25,* 159–171.

John Templeton Foundation. (1997). *1997–1998 honor roll for character-building colleges.* Radnor, PA: Author.

Keith-Spiegel, P. (1999). *Student attitudes toward instructor exam monitoring modes.* Unpublished manuscript, Ball State University.

Keith-Spiegel, P., & Gray-Shellberg, L. (1997). *Student awareness of academic honesty code content.* Unpublished manuscript, Ball State University.

Keith-Spiegel, P., Tabachnick, B. G., & Allen, M. (1993). Ethics in academia: Students' views of professors' actions. *Ethics & Behavior, 3,* 149–162.

Keith-Spiegel, P., Tabachnick, B. G., Whitley, B. E., Jr., & Washburn, J. (1998). Why do professors ignore cheating? Opinions of a national sample of psychology instructors. *Ethics & Behavior, 8,* 215–227.

Keith-Spiegel, P., Wittig, A. F., Perkins, D. V., Balogh, D. W., & Whitley, B. E., Jr. (1993). *The ethics of teaching: A casebook.* Muncie, IN: Ball State University Press.

Kerkvliet, J., & Sigmund, C. L. (1999). Can we control cheating in the classroom? *Journal of Economic Education, 30,* 331–343.

Kibler, W. L. (1993a). Academic dishonesty: A student development dilemma. *NASPA Journal, 30,* 252–267.

Kibler, W. L. (1993b). A framework for addressing academic dishonesty from a student development perspective. *NASPA Journal, 31,* 8–18.

Kibler, W. L. (1994). Addressing academic dishonesty: What are institutions of higher education doing and not doing? *NASPA Journal, 31,* 92–101.

Kibler, W. L., Nuss, E.M., Paterson, B. G., & Pavela, G. (1988). *Academic integrity and student development: Legal issues and policy perspectives.* Asheville, NC: College Administration Publications.

LaBeff, E. E., Clark, R. E., Haines, V. J., & Diekhoff, G. M. (1990). Situational ethics and college student cheating. *Sociological Inquiry, 60,* 190–198.

Lanza-Kaduce, L., & Klug, M. (1986). Learning to cheat: The interaction of moral-development and social learning theories. *Deviant Behavior, 7,* 243–259.

Law student arrested for hiring hit man. (1995, March 3). *Chronicle of Higher Education,* p. A6.

Livosky, M., & Tauber, R. T. (1994). Views of cheating among college students and faculty. *Psychology in the Schools, 31,* 72–82.

Lords, E. (2000, October 20). Minnesota charges 17 former basketball players with academic misconduct in cheating scandal. *Chronicle of Higher Education,* p. A54.

Maramark, S., & Maline, M. B. (1993). *Academic dishonesty among college students.* Washington, DC: U.S. Department of Education. (ERIC Document Reproduction Service No. ED 360 903)

McCabe, D. L. (1992). The influence of situational ethics on cheating among college students. *Sociological Inquiry, 62,* 365–374.

McCabe, D. L. (1993). Faculty responses to academic dishonesty: The influence of student honor codes. *Research in Higher Education, 34,* 647–658.

McCabe, D. L., & Trevino, L. K. (1993). Academic dishonesty: Honor codes and other contextual influences. *Journal of Higher Education, 64,* 522–538.

McCabe, D. L., & Trevino, L. K. (1995). Cheating among business students: A challenge for business leaders and educators. *Journal of Management Education, 19,* 205–218.

McCabe, D. L., Trevino, L. K., & Butterfield, K. D. (1996). The influence of collegiate and corporate codes of conduct on ethics-related behavior in the workplace. *Business Ethics Quarterly, 6,* 461–476.

McCabe, D. L., Trevino, L. K., & Butterfield, K. D. (1999). Academic integrity in honor code and non-honor code environments. *Journal of Higher Education, 70,* 211–234.

McCollum, K. (1996, August 2). Web site where students share term papers has professors worried about plagiarism. *Chronicle of Higher Education,* p. A28.

McLeod, S. H. (1992). Responding to plagiarism: The role of the WPA. *WPA: Writing Program Administration, 15*(3), 7–16.

Melendez, B. (1985). *Honor code study.* Faculty of Arts & Sciences Harvard University.

Michaels, J. W., & Miethe, T. D. (1989). Applying theories of deviance to academic cheating. *Social Science Quarterly, 70,* 870–885.

Moffatt, M. (1990). *Undergraduate cheating.* Unpublished manuscript, Department of Anthropology, Rutgers University. (ERIC Document Reproduction Service No. ED 334 921)

Morgan, B. L., Korschgen, A. J., & Gardner, J. C. (1996, August). *Students' and professors' views on the ethics of faculty behavior.* Paper presented at the annual meeting of the American Psychological Association, Toronto, Canada.

Mowday, R. T. (1991). Equity theory predictions of behavior in organizations. In R. M. Steers & L. W. Porter (Eds.), *Motivation and work behavior* (5th ed., pp. 111–131). New York. McGraw-Hill.

Nuss, E. M. (1984). Academic integrity: Comparing faculty and student attitudes. *Improving College and University Teaching, 32,* 140–144.

Ory, J.C., & Ryan, K. E. (1993). *Tips for improving testing and grading.* Newbury Park, CA: Sage.

Paine, L. S. (1994). Managing for organizational integrity. *Harvard Business Review, 72*(2), 106–117.

Paldy, L. G. (1996). The problem that won't go away: Addressing the causes of cheating. *Journal of College Science Teaching, 26,* 4–6.

Pavela, G. (1978). Judicial review of academic decision-making after Horowitz. *School Law Journal, 55*(8), 55–75.

Pavela, G. (1997a). Applying the power of association on campus: A model code of academic integrity. *Journal of College and University Law, 24,* 97–118.

Pavela, G. (1997b). Disciplinary and academic decisions pertaining to students: A review of 1996 decisions. *Journal of College and University Law, 24,* 213–224.

Pavela, G., & McCabe, D. (1993). The surprising return of honor codes. *Planning for Higher Education, 21*(Summer), 27–32

Peyser, M. (1992, January 6). A cheater's guide to high marks (And big $). *Newsweek, 123,* p. 45.

Pulvers, K., & Diekhoff, G. M. (1999). The relationship between academic dishonesty and college classroom environment. *Research in Higher Education, 40,* 487–498.

Randall, M. E. (1998). Can the academic integrity of cost-effective distance learning course offerings be protected? In D. D. Barnett, L. Rudolph, & K. O. Clifford (Eds.), *Academic integrity matters* (pp. 125–133). Washington, DC: National Association of Student Personnel Administrators.

Risacher, J., & Slonaker, W. (1996). Academic misconduct: NASPA institutional members' views and a pragmatic model policy. *NASPA Journal, 33,* 105–124.

Robinson, J. (1992, October). *International students and American university culture: Adjustment issues.* Paper presented at the meeting of the Washington Area Teachers of English to Speakers of Other Languages, Arlington, VA. (ERIC Document Reproduction Service No. ED 350 968)

Rodabaugh, R. C. (1996). Institutional commitment to fairness in college teaching. In L. Fisch (Ed.), *Ethical dimensions of college and university teaching* (pp. 37–45). San Francisco: Jossey-Bass.

Roig, M. (1997). Can undergraduate students determine whether text has been plagiarized? *Psychological Record, 47,* 113–122.

Roig, M. (1999). When college students' attempts at paraphrasing become instances of potential plagiarism. *Psychological Reports, 84,* 973–982.

Roig, M., & Ballew, C. (1994). Attitudes toward cheating of self and others by college students and professors. *Psychological Record, 44,* 3–12.

Rosenfeld, L. B. (1983). Communication climate and coping mechanisms in the college classroom. *Communication Education, 32,* 167–174.

Roth, N. L., & McCabe, D. L. (1995). Communication strategies for addressing academic dishonesty. *Journal of College Student Development, 36,* 531–541.

Saltman, P. (1996). Cheating prevention: Not an end in itself. *Journal of College Science Teaching, 26,* 5.

Sandeen, A. (1985). The legacy of values education in college student personnel work. In J. C. Dalton (Ed.), *Promoting values development in college students* (pp. 1–15). Washington, DC: National Association of Student Personnel Administrators.

Schein, E. H. (1985). *Organizational culture and leadership.* San Francisco: Jossey-Bass.

Schneider, A. (1999, January 22). Why professors don't do more to stop students who cheat. *Chronicle of Higher Education,* pp. A8–A10.

Shen, F. (1989). The classroom and the wider culture: Identity as a key to learning English composition. *College Composition and Communication, 40,* 459–466.

Sierles, F. S., Kushner, B. D., & Krause, P. B. (1988). A controlled experiment with a medical school student honor system. *Journal of Medical Education, 63,* 705–712.

Sims, R. L. (1993). The relationship between academic dishonesty and unethical business practices. *Journal of Education for Business, 68,* 207–211.

Sims, R. L. (1995). The severity of academic dishonesty: A comparison of faculty and student views. *Psychology in the Schools, 32,* 233–238.

Singhal, A. C. (1982). Factors in students' dishonesty. *Psychological Reports, 51,* 775–780.

Singhal, A. C., & Johnson, P. (1983). How to halt student dishonesty. *College Student Journal, 17,* 13–19.

Stern, E. B., & Havlicek, L. (1986). Academic misconduct: Results of faculty and undergraduate student surveys. *Journal of Allied Health, 15,* 129–142.

Sutton, E. M., & Huba, M. E. (1995). Undergraduate student perceptions of academic dishonesty as a function of ethnicity and religious participation. *NASPA Journal, 33,* 19–34.

Sykes, C. J. (1988). *ProfScam: Professors and the demise of higher education.* Washington, DC: Regnery Gateway.

Tabachnick, B. G., Keith-Spiegel, P., & Pope, K. S. (1991). Ethics of teaching: Beliefs and behaviors of psychologists as educators. *American Psychologist, 46,* 506–515.

Tigwell, K. (1987). The crib card examination system. *Assessment and Evaluation in Higher Education, 12,* 56–65.

Tittle, C. R., & Rowe, A. R. (1973). Moral appeal, sanction threat, and deviance: An experimental test. *Social Forces, 20,* 488–498.

Tom, G., & Borin, N. (1988). Cheating in academe. *Journal of Education for Business, 63,* 153–157.

Trevino, L. K. (1990). A cultural perspective on changing and developing organizational ethics. *Research in Organizational Change and Development, 4,* 195–230.

U.S. Naval Academy. (1997, June 6). *United States Naval Academy Honor Remediation Program* [Information paper posted on the World Wide Web]. Annapolis, MD: Author. Retrieved July 7, 1997, from the World Wide Web: http://www.nadn.navy.mil/CharacterDevelopment/honor/remed.html.

Whitley, B. E., Jr. (1996). Does "cheating" help? The effect of using authorized crib notes during examinations. *College Student Journal, 30,* 489–493.

Whitley, B. E., Jr. (1998). Factors associated with cheating among college students: A review. *Research in Higher Education, 39,* 235–274.

Whitley, B. E., Jr., & Kite, M. E. (1998). The classroom environment and academic integrity: A behavioral science perspective. In D. D. Barnett, L. Rudolph, & K. O. Clifford (Eds), *Academic integrity matters* (pp. 39–56). Washington, DC: National Association of Student Personnel Administrators.

Whitley, B. E., Jr., & Kost, C. R. (1999). College students' perceptions of peers who cheat. *Journal of Applied Social Psychology, 29,* 1732–1759.

Wilcox, J. R., & Ebbs, S. L. (1992). *The leadership compass: Values and ethics in higher education.* ASHE-ERIC Higher Education Report No. 1. Washington, DC: George Washington University, School of Education and Human Development.

Wilhoit, S. (1994). Helping students avoid plagiarism. *College Teaching, 42,* 161–164.

Wilson, R. (1998, July 31). Professor says UCLA retaliated against him for reporting cheating incident. *Chronicle of Higher Education,* p. A9.

Wryobeck, J. M., & Whitley, B. E., Jr. (1999). Educational value orientation and peer perception of cheaters. *Ethics & Behavior, 9,* 231–242.

Author Index

Subject Index